THE SCARLET LETTER

A Verse Tragedy In Two Acts By
D. A. Dorwart

Based Upon The Novel By

Nathaniel Hawthorne

BookLocker

Published by BookLocker.com, Inc., St. Petersburg, Florida.

Printed on acid-free paper.

The characters and events in this book are fictitious. Any similarity to real persons, living or dead, is coincidental and not intended by the author.

First Edition

CAUTION: Professionals and amateurs are hereby warned that all material in this book, being fully protected under the copyright laws of the United States and other countries, is subject to royalty. Worldwide stage rights are controlled exclusively by the author. No professional or non-professional performance of this play may be given without obtaining in advance the written permission from the author and his representative and paying the requisite fee. Please contact the author's representative at Abrams Artists Agency, 275 Seventh Avenue, 26th Floor, New York, NY 10001 (646) 486-4600, Attn: Ron Gwiazda.

Library of Congress Cataloging in Publication Data
Dorwart, D.A.
The Scarlet Letter by D.A. Dorwart
Library of Congress Control Number: 2020905525

"One loses one's classics. Oh, not all. A part.
A part remains. That is what I find so wonderful,
a part remains of one's classics to help one
through the day."

Winnie in Samuel Beckett's **Happy Days**

The *Scarlet Letter* was first presented in the SDC Foundation staged reading series at Lincoln Center in New York City and was the winner of a John Golden Award. Subsequent readings were held at CAP 21 and the Acting Studio. All presentations were directed by the author and had the following cast.

CAST

HESTER PRYNNE	Maryann Plunkett
ROGER CHILLINGSWORTH	Jay O. Sanders
ARTHUR DIMMESDALE	Stephen Turner
JOHN WILSON	Denis Holmes
ELIZABETH/MISTRESS HIBBINS	Aideen O'Kelly
JOHN THOMAS/JAILOR	Peter Francis James
GOVENOR BELLINGHAM	William Meisle
CHORUS/MARTHA	Tod Randolph
SARAH	Seana Kofoed
ABIGAIL	Jackie Farrington
PEARL	Emily Chepiga
BEADLE	Allen Kennedy
JOHN THOMAS/BRACKETT/CAPTAIN	Curt Hostetter

ॐ ॐ

The
Scarlet Letter

CAST

(in order of appearance)

CHORUS	A woman, descendant of Hester Prynne
ELIZABETH	A woman of advanced years
MARTHA THOMAS	A townswoman
SARAH	A young townswoman
ABIGAIL	A young townswoman
JOHN THOMAS	Martha's husband
TOWN BEADLE	A minor parish official
HESTER PRYNNE	A young woman and mother of Pearl
ROGER CHILLINGSWORTH	Hester's husband, the Leech
JOHN WILSON	The senior minister
GOVERNOR BELLINGHAM	An elderly gentleman
ARTHUR DIMMESDALE	A young minister Hester's lover
BRACKETT	The Jailer
MISTRESS HIBBINS	Bellingham's sister, the "Witch"
PEARL	A girl of three (non-speaking) A girl of around eight
SHIP CAPTAIN	A Spaniard

TOWNSFOLK (non-speaking)
  Algonquin/Nipmuck(s)
  Soldiers
  Tradesmen
  Children, *etc.*

Note: *All of the characters, except for the Ship Captain, speak with English accents. Excluding the Native American(s) and the children, the characters are first generation English immigrants, "born and bred in the time of Elizabeth I" and James I.* They have lived in exile as refugees in Leiden, the Netherlands for over a decade. It may be possible, therefore, that one or two are Dutch. Their accents reflect regionalisms as well as education and economic station.*

* Descriptions in quotes are taken directly from Hawthorne.

TIME
The Mid-Seventeenth Century

PLACE
In and Around the King's Colony of Boston, Massachusetts

ACT ONE

The set consists of a mammoth wooden wall upstage rising from the stage floor up into the flies. The wall is weathered and stained to permit projections that dramatically change its nature. The wall contains several doors, flush with its surface and barely discernible. There are, for example, two massive doors center, within which is a smaller door. There are also doors left and right – as needed. On a second level are sliding panels that open to create balconies. A lone small window with leaded mullions appears near the extreme top right side of the wall. The stage floor is raked and surrounded with wood chips.

At rise: Percussion/Music. The cast assembles briskly in a formal arrangement across the stage. They are anonymous, perhaps silhouetted, and motionless. A spot picks up the Chorus, a striking woman dressed in deep crimson garb, a gown or suit abstracted, modernized as are all the costumes.

Prologue

CHORUS

> A throng of men and women in somber hue,
> With beards and steeple hats and muslin hoods,
> Assembles here before this prison door.
> The grim aspect of their facade portends
> A dreadful undertaking's close at hand.
> Nearon the threshold of this my narrative,
> Which issues forth from that unlucky portal,
> There stands a rose. It has been kept alive
> In history, surviv'd the wilderness
> Long after pine and oak have abdicated;
> 'Tis cover'd now, this month of June, with gems
> According fragrance and fragile beauty,
> A token showing Nature's deepest heart
> Can still be kind to the outlaw coming forth.
> To you, the listener, one flower tender'd here
> As sweet and moral blossom or as relief
> To a tale of human frailty and abject grief.

Scene One

Music/Sound. The lights quickly cross fade. It is now morning, and the impatient crowd buzzes in the square outside the prison. A group of women gathers downstage. They are "countrywomen, broad-shouldered and ruddy-cheeked, bold and rotund of speech." Sarah is the youngest, and Elizabeth, the matriarch, is the oldest.

ELIZABETH

      I tell ye, it would greatly be to public
      Benefit if we good wives of fair
      Repute should handle Hester Prynne. If hussy
      Such as she before us stood for judgement,
      Would she receive a sentence like
      The magistrates awarded her? Marry,
      I trow not!

MARTHA

                  They say, the Reverend Master
      Dimmesdale takes it grievously to heart
      Such scandal comes upon his congregation.

ABIGAIL

      The magistrates are God-fearing men
      But merciful overmuch.

ELIZABETH and SARAH

                         Aye. 'Tis true.

ABIGAIL

      They should have branded her with iron
      Hot upon her brow. Yea, Madame Hester
      Would have winc'd at that, I warrant me.

SARAH

      Little will she care what they put upon
      The bodice of her gown. She'll cover it
      With brooch or bib and walk the streets as ever.

MARTHA
>But let her cover it as best she may,
>The sting will always be within her heart.

ELIZABETH
>Why do we talk of brands on gown or flesh?
>This woman's brought us shame and ought to die!

JOHN THOMAS (*crossing to Martha*)
>Mercy on you, Elizabeth! Is there
>No virtue in woman save that which springs from fear
>Of gallows? Harsh words. Mark ye, now,
>The lock is turning in the prison door,
>And Mistress Prynne comes forth into the light.

ELIZABETH
>The magistrates will have themselves to pay
>If their own wives and daughters go astray.

The small center door opens from within. Like a black shadow emerging into the sun, the Town-Beadle, staff of office in hand, comes forth. He lays a hand upon the arm of a tall woman and draws her forward to the threshold of the prison-door. With a natural dignity, she repels his hand and steps forward into the sunlight. She carries a baby in her arms and shields it from the burning light. She surveys the townspeople and lowers the baby to reveal on the breast of her gown, in crimson cloth, surrounded by embroidered flourishes of gold, the scarlet letter 'A'.

JOHN THOMAS
>Three months have not diminish'd her in beauty.

MARTHA
>Rather bathes she in misfortune's halo.

SARAH
>She has good skill at needle, that is sure.

ELIZABETH
>Did ever brazen plot such exhibition?
>Her manner flaunts the crime before our faces.

ABIGAIL
> And makes a pride from that the magistrates
> Had well resolv'd a fitting punishment.

MARTHA
> Good neighbors, peace. Let's not add rank
> To this e'er-growing spectacle. I know
> That every stitch in that embroidered letter,
> She's doubtless felt engrav'd upon her heart.

BEADLE (*pounding with his staff*)
> In the name of good King Charles, make way!
> Open wide a passage! I promise Mistress
> Prynne shall be install'd where all may have
> Fair sight of her, from rise to setting sun.
> A blessing on our righteous Colony,
> Where iniquity is dragg'd into the light.
> Come, Hester Prynne, and show your scarlet
> Letter about the square for all to see.

Children run before the Beadle and Hester. The crowd falls in behind them as they create a procession. Apart from the crowd stand a native warrior and his companion, Roger Chillingsworth, a man of great intensity and mystery. He has a slight limp. As Hester passes him, her gaze becomes transfixed. The procession exits, and Chillingsworth intercepts John Thomas. Martha and his child(ren) wait apart briefly for him, then exit after the crowd.)

CHILLINGSWORTH
> Kind sir, a moment please. Who is this woman?
> Wherefore is she paraded to such public shame?

JOHN THOMAS
> You must be a stranger hereabout, good sir,
> Else you'd have heard of Hester Prynne, for she
> Hath rais'd a goodly scandal.

CHILLINGSWORTH
> How so, pray tell?

CHILLINGSWORTH (*cont'd.*)
>I am a stranger, truly sir, a wanderer
>Against my will. With mishap have I met
>And long resided 'mong the native-folk;
>Just now deliver'd here by this good man.
>So please tell me about this Hester Prynne.
>Have I her name correctly? What's her offense?

JOHN THOMAS
>'Twill glad your heart aft' your predicament
>To find a place wherein transgression's punished,
>As here in our god-loving colony.
>Yon' woman was wife to a learned man,
>English by birth, who plann'd to cross the sea
>And cast his lot with us in Massachusetts.
>He sent his wife ahead and stay'd at home
>Dispensing his affairs. In two years since
>No tidings come of this poor gentleman, and,
>Thus, the wife was left to her misguidance.

CHILLINGSWORTH
>So learned a man might've thought more learnedly.
>Perhaps he'll come to look into the matter.

JOHN THOMAS.
>It behooves him well, if he be still in life.
>More like he rests upon the salt sea's bed.

CHILLINGSWORTH
>The babe appears some three or four months old.
>Pray tell, kind sir, who may the father be?

JOHN THOMAS
>With that I cannot help. The matter stays
>A riddle, for Mistress Prynne declines to speak.
>Perhaps the guilty stands as witness there,
>Unknown to man, forgetting he's observ'd by God.

John Thomas' son or daughter runs in to fetch his father.

CHILLINGSWORTH
>And the punishment decreed for this offense?

JOHN THOMAS
>The penalty is death.

CHILLINGSWORTH
>>Death, you say?

JOHN THOMAS
>Our magistrates have not been bold to put
>In force the absolute of our just law.
>With tenderness of heart, they have decreed
>She stand this day upon the pillory,
>And for the rest of her remaining days,
>To wear a mark of shame upon her bosom.

CHILLINGSWORTH
>A wise decree.

JOHN THOMAS
>>Indeed, sir, yes. And now –

John Thomas' bows courteously and then exits with his child. Chillingsworth and the warrior stand alone.

CHILLINGSWORTH (*augmenting with sign language*)
>She'll be a living sermon 'gainst such sin
>Until the letter's carv'd upon her tomb.
>And yet a wife so young and fair was doubtless
>Tempted to her fall. Iniquity's companion
>Should stand beside her on the pillory
>And take the shame upon her breast upon his own.
>He will be known, I vow. He will be known!

They exit.

Scene Two

The lights cross fade as the procession enters. A platform rises upon which stands a pillory. The balcony doors slide open above to reveal Governor Bellingham, magistrates and two ministers, the senior John Wilson and the younger Arthur Dimmesdale. The Beadle attempts to help Hester up the steps of the platform, but she, again, refuses his assistance. When she reaches the top she turns toward the assembly.

WILSON (*first silencing the crowd*)
>Hearken unto me, Hester Prynne!
>I've sought in vain to sway my younger brethren
>That he should deal with you, herein the face
>Of Heaven and all before us now assembl'd.
>Knowing your native temper more than I,
>Better could he assess what arguments
>That might prevail upon your obstinacy
>And unbefitting stance, insomuch
>As you no longer should conceal the name
>Of him who tempted you to this most grievous fall.
>With young man's softness, he opposes;
>Saying it would wrong a woman's nature, forcing
>Her by light of day before a gather'd
>Host to bare her heart's abysmal secrets.
>But I assert, the shame lay in the sin's
>Commission, not the showing forth of it.
>Therefore, brother Dimmesdale, I beseech you,
>Yet again, to argue for this sinner's soul.

He turns to Bellingham to enlist support.

BELLINGHAM
>Master Dimmesdale, responsibility
>Of this poor woman's soul abides with you.
>Admonish her confession as proof and
>Consequence thereof.

WILSON

>Speak brother. It is
>Of magnitude to her soul, as well to thine,
>Within whose charge she rests. Pray, convince
>This woman to tell the truth!

Dimmesdale reluctantly rises and comes forward.

DIMMESDALE.

>Mistress Prynne,
>Hears't thou what these good men direct? See'st thou
>The grave accountability under which I labor?
>If thou believ'st it be for thy soul's peace,
>And that thy earthly punishment thereby
>Be more effectual to your salvation,
>Then I charge thee now speak out the name
>Of him, your fellow sinner and fellow suff'rer.
>Be not still from any misdirected
>Tenderness, though he descend from high
>And stand by thee on shame's own pedestal,
>Yet were it better than to hide a guilty
>Conscience through his life. What can this silence
>Do for him, except to add hypocrisy
>To sin? Heaven hath granted thee
>An open ignominy so thou may'st exercise
>An open triumph over evil.
>Take heed how thou deniest him, who lacks
>The courage here to grasp it for himself,
>The bitter cup present'd to thy lips!

Silence

WILSON

>Woman! Transgress ye not beyond the limits
>Of Heaven's mercy! Speak out the name!
>Thy repentance may avail to cleave
>The scarlet letter from thy breast. Speak!

HESTER
>Ye sir cannot remove it. It is
>Too deeply branded. And would that I might so
>Endure his agony as well as mine.

ELIZABETH
>Speak, the name!

CROWD (*becoming agitated*)
>Yes. Speak. Speak his name!

ABIGAIL (*shouting.*)
>Give your child a father!

CROWD
>Speak. Speak.
>Speak his name!

HESTER
>Never! Never will I speak his name!

DIMMESDALE (*aside*)
>She will not speak. What wondrous
>Strength and generosity.

CROWD (*chanting and yelling*)
>Speak. Speak. The father's name. Speak!

DIMMESDALE
>And still she will not speak!

HESTER (*above the din*)
>In heaven my child will find his father to come.
>NEVER SHALL SHE DESCRY AN EARTHLY ONE!

The lights fade to black as the shouts continue.

Scene Three

The prison. The area is divided into a corridor and Hester's cell. In the blackout, moaning is heard, then the crying of a baby. The lights come up on jailer Brackett, who is leading Chillingsworth toward the cell.

BRACKETT (*angrily*)
>She hath been like a soul possess'd, demanding
>Constant watchfulness lest she encourage
>Mischief to herself or to the babe.
>Not rebuke nor threats of punishment
>Have quell'd her insubordination.

CHILLINGSWORTH
>You have done well, good sir, to send for me.
>Fear not, you shall have peace herein this night.

BRACKETT
>Nay, if your worship can accomplish that
>I'll own you are a man of skill indeed
>And far advanc'd of any hereabout.
>There lacks but little I should take in hand
>To drive the Devil out of her with stripes.

CHILLINGSWORTH
>Prithee, leave me with my patient, now.
>I promise you that Mistress Prynne shall be
>Amenable to your authority.

Brackett hesitates, then exits. The lights come up in the cell. A disheveled Hester is on the bed rocking and moaning. The baby is wrapped and lying on a trundle bed crying. Chillingsworth enters the cell. Hester stops rocking. They stare at each other momentarily, and then Chillingsworth turns his attention to the baby. After examining it, he removes a powder from a leather case and places it in a mug. He then adds water.

>These past two year's sojourn and studies 'mong
>The Native tribes, versed in properties
>Of herbs and roots, have made a better healer
>Now of me than many claiming medical degrees.

Offering her the cup.

>Here, take this. The child is yours.

CHILLINGSWORTH (*cont'd.*)
    It will not recognize my aspect nor
    My voice. Therefore, administer this draft,
    With thine own hand. Come take the cup.

HESTER (*not taking the cup*)
    Wouldst thou avenge thyself on innocence?

CHILLINGSWORTH
    Foolish woman. What should trouble me
    To harm this misbegotten babe? The mixture's
    Potent but for good. Were it my child – mine own
    As well as thine – I could no better tend.

Hester does not move. Chillingsworth takes the infant in his arms and administers the brew. The baby soon grows quiet. Chillingsworth replaces the baby on the trundle and turns his attention to Hester. After examining her eyes and taking her pulse, he mixes another draught.

    Many secrets I have learn'd afield
    Here's recipe, less soothing than a sinless conscience,
    For that I can't afford, but it will calm
    Thy passion's swell and heaving. Come, drink!

HESTER
    I have thought of death. Have wish'd for it.
    Would have pray'd for it, were't fit that such
    As I should pray for any thing. Yet, if death
    Be in this cup, I bid thee think again –

CHILLINGSWORTH
    Dost thou know me so little, Hester Prynne?
    Are my purposes so shallow? If my
    Imagination schem'd some vengeance, what could
    I plot that's better than to let thee live
    And let this burning shame upon thy bosom blaze.

Pause.

CHILLINGSWORTH (*cont'd.*)
>Live and bear about thy doom with thee,
>In men's and women's eyes, in yonder child's
>Eyes, and in the eyes of him whom thou
>Didst once call husband.

Hester hesitates and then drains the mug. Chillingsworth takes the stool and sits across from her. Pause.

>I ask not wherefore hast thou transgressed;
>The cause, it lies no further than this cell.
>It was my folly as well thy weakness. I was
>A man of letters, book-worm to libraries,
>Who gave his years to feed the hungry dream
>Of knowledge. A man already in decay.
>What had I to do with youth and beauty
>Like thine own? Deform'd from birth, how could
>I fool myself, that intellectual
>Gifts might veil deformity from a young
>Girl's sight? Men call me wise, but was
>A sage e'er wise on his behalf? The moment
>We descended chapel steps, I should
>Have seen that scarlet letter looming forth
>To mark the end of our ordained path.

HESTER
>From very first, I was frank with thee.
>I felt no love.

CHILLINGSWORTH
>>True. It was my folly.
>I have conceded it.

HESTER
>>Nor feign'd I any.

CHILLINGSWORTH
>But up till then, my world had been so cheerless.
>My heart a habitation large enough

CHILLINGSWORTH (*cont'd.*)
    For many guests, but vacant and lonely, without
    A household fire. I ach'd to kindle one.
    'Twas not so wild a dream – though old I was,
    And dull I was, and crippl'd too – the simple
    Bliss dispersed so far and wide for all
    Mankind might yet be mine. And, thus, I
    Welcom'd thee into my heart, into
    Its inmost chamber, longing so to warm
    Thee by the flame thy presence kindled there.

HESTER
    I have greatly wronged thee.

CHILLINGSWORTH
                          We've wrong'd each other.
    Mine was the first when I betray'd thy budding
    Youth into unnatural alliance
    With my decay. Therefore, I seek no vengeance;
    I plot no evil 'gainst thee. 'Tween us the scale
    Hangs balanc'd. But, Hester, the man still lives
    Who wrong'd us both. I'd have his name.

HESTER
    Ask me not, I pray.

CHILLINGSWORTH
                      For mercy's sake, I must.
    And so, again, I ask, who is the man?

HESTER
    And I, again, reply, ask me not.

CHILLINGSWORTH
    Thou wilt deny me yet again?
    Not so. I'll have this villain's name!

HESTER (*vehemently*)
    Thou shalt never know his name!

D. A. Dorwart

CHILLINGSWORTH
'Never know him,' thou sayest? 'Never?'
Believe me, Hester, few things, be they in the outward
World or thought's invisible domain,
Few things remain conceal'd from him who
Dedicates his self to solving mystery.
Thou mayest conceal him from the multitude,
Thou mayest conceal him from the magistrates,
Thou mayest conceal him from the ministers,
But I embrace this quest with greater purpose,
With greater faculties than all before possess'd.
I seek this man as I have sought the truth
In books, as gold in alchemy. There is
A sympathy 'tween us will make me conscious.
He'll sigh, and I shall feel myself exhale.
He'll quake, and I shall feel myself quiver.
He bears no mark of sin upon his gown
But I shall read it sure upon his heart.
And be it soon or late, he will be mine!
Fear not that I shall interfere with heaven's
Retribution or betray him to the law.
Nor shall I plot against his life nor 'gainst
His fame, as he must be of fair repute.
Let him live! Let him hide himself
In outward reverence, if he may.
Come the end, he will be mine!

HESTER
Thy acts are like mercy. Thy words are terror.

CHILLINGSWORTH
One thing, thou that was my wife, I urge.
You've kept thy paramour's secret;
Keep, likewise, mine! Breathe not to any
Human soul that thou e'er call'd me husband.
On this untamed outskirts, I'll pitch my tent,
Elsewhere a wanderer, sequester'd from

CHILLINGSWORTH (*cont'd.*)
>Humanity. But here I find a woman,
>Child, and man amongst whom there exists
>The closest ligaments. No matter they
>Of love or hate, or right or wrong, from this
>Day on, thou and thine belong to me.
>My home is where thou art. Betray me not.

HESTER
>Why not announce thyself and cast me off?

CHILLINGSWORTH
>Because I'll suffer not the disrepute
>Besmirching the husband of a faithless woman.
>Nor will I stand beside you pilloried
>For all to see upon a pedestal of shame.
>It is my plan to live and die unknown.
>Let me be as one already dead.
>Know me not by word nor look, and breathe
>Not this confidence to thy accomplice.
>His fame, his post, his life are in my hands.

HESTER
>I'll keep thy secret, as I have harbor'd his.

CHILLINGSWORTH
>Swear to it!

HESTER
>I swear, as God's my witness.

CHILLINGSWORTH
>My bus'ness then's accomplish'd. Alone I leave
>Thee now with child and with thy scarlet letter.

He starts to leave but turns back and smiles.

>How is it, Hester? Doth thy sentence
>Bind thee wear the mark e'en in thy sleep?
>Art thou not feared of dreams and nightmares?

15

HESTER

> Why dost thou smile at me like that?
> Hast thou enticed me into a bond will prove
> The very ruin of this soul of mine?

CHILLINGSWORTH

> Not thy soul, Hester Prynne. No, not thine.

He exits. The lights fade.

Scene Four

The waiting room of the prison. Wilson is followed onstage by a reluctant Dimmesdale.

WILSON

> The term of her confinement's now at end,
> And if she means to stay –

DIMMESDALE.

> What mean you, 'if?'

WILSON

> There's no restrictive clause in her reproof
> To keep within the settlement's confines,
> And if she means to stay and live 'mongst us,
> We must, for child's sake, be vigilant.
> With unattended walk from prison door
> Begins her daily custom that by strength
> Of nature she must bear or sink beneath.

DIMMESDALE

> Hath she not shown combative energy
> That so enabl'd her to turn the scene
> Of spectacle to one of lurid triumph?

WILSON

> It was an insulated 'fair to meet
> She rous'd unnatural strength of nerves.
> Tomorrow will bring a greater tribulation

WILSON (*cont'd.*)
>And so, as well, the next day and the next.
>The accumulating months and added years
>Amassing misery upon the heap of shame.
>The magistrates will keep a watch o'er her,
>But our concern transcends the temporal
>To oversee the twosome's spiritual guidance
>And how her act reflects upon our flock.
>She must become the symbol at which we point
>Embodying sinful lust and Eve's own frailty.

DIMMESDALE
>Is she not a wayward in the eyes of God,
>Who should receive our pity, not our scorn?
>Does one immoral act obliterate all else,
>That she's no more nor less than this one sin?
>Will this infamy she carries thither
>Be her only monument in life?

WILSON
>She's broken God's commandant. As such
>Her daily torture will absolve her soul
>And forge a purity beyond the natural
>Innocence in which she first was born.

Hester, carrying the baby in her arms, enters with Brackett.

DIMMESDALE
>Your counsel is my guide in these affairs.

WILSON
>Master Brackett, The Reverend Master Dimmesdale
>And I have come to speak with Mistress Prynne
>Before she is discharg'd from out your keep.

BRACKETT (*not withdrawing*)
>So please, your reverends.

WILSON
>   In private, man.

BRACKETT

> I'll wait nearby, should you have need of me.

He begrudgingly withdraws upstage and waits.

WILSON

> Mistress, we come to make inquiry of your
> Intentions.

HESTER

> I have but good intentions, sir.

WILSON

> No doubt, but we must ask about your plans.
> What provisions have you devis'd for the child?
> Do you intend to stay within the settlement?

HESTER

> I had no other thought.

WILSON

> Why do you choose
> To stay when you are free to go? Why not
> Restore to England, your place of birth, or hide
> Yourselves in Holland?

HESTER

> I've no intention, sir, of hiding.
> My sin's the root which strikes into this soil.
> Here hath been the scene of my disgrace;
> Here shall be the scene of my rebuke.

WILSON

> No other reason binds you here?

HESTER (*pause*)

> None, sir.

WILSON

> Very well. The course you choose removes you from
> The sphere of human charities. Have you
> Considered where the two of you shall lodge?

HESTER
>I have us'd what little fortune still
>Remains and taken refuge, a lonesome cottage
>Looking west across the bay and just
>Within the verge of the peninsula, but not
>In close vicinity to other habitation.

WILSON
>I know the place of which you speak. The soil
>About is much too sterile for cultivation.
>How do you plan to feed yourself as well the child?

HESTER
>We will manage. Our needs are simple.

WILSON
>Simple though they be, one needs to eat,
>And must not count to live by charity.

HESTER
>I'll be no burden upon society.
>No thing I seek to gain beyond subsistence.
>I hold the art – were better called a craft –
>Of needlepoint. A specimen of this
>Imagination lies here upon my breast.

WILSON
>Need I point out that you are in a land
>Providing little scope for its demand.

HESTER
>It shall suffice. Though now there be infrequent
>Call for my endeavor's finer work,
>Yet by degree it may be otherwise.
>And as no other hereabouts enjoys
>Such skill, I trust to fill this vacancy.

WILSON
>We've cast behind the past's extravagances.
>The law, it binds us to simplicity.

HESTER

> And for myself, I ask no less than that.
> Yet for the man of rank and wealth, upon
> Assuming power's rein, an outward show
> Of his position's deem'd necessity.
> A magistrate's inauguration calls
> For emblematic proof of his official
> State – as well a minister's ordaining.
> Your own embroider'd gloves and bands bear witness
> Advocating what I say –

WILSON

> Yes, well...

HESTER

> And what array there is for common funerals,
> As well for robes afford'd every
> Babe new born –

WILSON

> Yes, yes. Very well.
> We're satisfied and need not press the issue.

HESTER

> Then if it please your Reverends, as this
> Affair is clos'd, am I now free to go?

Wilson nods assent, and Hester starts toward Brackett.

DIMMESDALE (*apologetically*)

> It is for the child's sake we have inquir'd.

HESTER (*turning back*)

> The child, my Pearl – for I have nam'd her so –
> My Pearl will want for no thing on this earth.
> I may be destin'd for a life with little pleasure,
> But she's God's gift, her mother's only treasure.

Hester exits, followed off by Brackett. As the lights cross fade, Wilson and Dimmesdale walk toward the parlor where a seated Chillingsworth waits.

Scene Five

WILSON
>The health of our good colony has hitherto
>Remain'd within a poor apothecary's
>Stewardship. The skillful man
>Of medicine's a rare occurrence hereabouts.

DIMMESDALE (*with light sarcasm*)
>Ah, yes, his advent has the air of mystery,
>As if he dropp'd full blown from out the sky.

WILSON
>A physician of his ability's a brilliant
>Acquisition. He's well acquainted with
>The scientific minds in Europe. Moreover,
>Appears exemplary in spiritual life.

DIMMESDALE
>But why come here? What could he, whose sphere
>Was in great cities, seek in our course wilderness?

WILSON
>Perhaps divine decree transports him here
>To care for our dear ailing minister.

DIMMESDALE
>Heaven rarely furthers its design with aim
>Toward stage-effect of what is called miraculous.

WILSON
>Even you cannot deny that there's
>A providential hand in such an opportune
>Arrival. You must make trial of this
>Physician's offer'd skill.

They enter the parlor and sit opposite Chillingsworth. Pause.

WILSON
>My colleague here, though young and of retiring
>Disposition, is an heaven-ordain'd
>Apostle. He's destin'd to do great deeds
>For our new colony as the church fathers
>Worked for early Christendom.

CHILLINGSWORTH
>Then, as I shall counsel his infirmity.
>So you, good Master Dimmesdale, shall from this day
>Abide as my religious beacon.

Pause. Wilson tries again to promote conversation.

WILSON
>The pallor of his cheek results from his extreme
>Devotion, both to sacred studies and his
>Parochial duties. I fear as well the frequent
>Practice of his fasts and nightly vigils –

DIMMESDALE
>I must keep the grossness of this earthly state
>From overshadowing my spiritual lamp.

WILSON (*half teasing*)
>If you should die, 'tis cause enough this world's
>Not worthy to be trod upon by your two feet.

DIMMESDALE (*rising and stepping apart*)
>If Providence should see it fit to beckon me,
>'Tis only due to my unworthiness
>To execute its mission here on earth.

CHILLINGSWORTH (*to Wilson, confidentially*)
>I wish to know the man before I try
>To do him good. Where lies a fervent heart
>And intellect, there corporeal disease
>Is ting'd with these peculiarities.
>I sense in him alert imagination
>And sensibility so intense

CHILLINGSWORTH (*cont'd.*)
>That bodily infirmity would likely
>Have its groundwork there. I must,
>As such, delve deep into your patient's heart,
>Explore his principles and recollection.
>Thereby, may I restore ordain'd perfection.

Scene Six

Music. Hester enters below with Pearl, who is now some three years old. The girl's dress is the same deep color as Hester's scarlet letter. Hester has with her a basket of wild roses. She plays briefly with Pearl as she puts the child to bed. The Townswomen are revealed at their labors in the balcony above.

ABIGAIL
>She hath purchased the richest tissues
>Made for children's dress and lets imagination
>Its full play in decorating them.
>Then, hand in hand, they traipse abroad
>Without a care, parading them in public.

SARAH
>Better the imp were clad in rustic weeds.

MARTHA
>Her own dress, though, is made from coarsest fabric.
>It is of hue most drab and bears but that
>One ornament which is her doom to wear.

ABIGAIL
>That ornament, lest you forget, goodwife,
>Is stain'd with sin against our Holy Father.
>To dress the child in its red hue affronts
>Both us and our dear Savior.

MARTHA
>Except the small expense upon the child
>She offers up sincerest sacrifice,

MARTHA (*cont'd.*)
> Sewing clothes for sick and poor, bestowing
> All her means in common charity.

ABIGAIL
> A paltry penance for such a swollen crime.

All but Martha snigger at the pun.

MARTHA (*quoting*)
> 'The giving hand, though foul, shall have fair praise.'

ELIZABETH (*sternly*)
> You miss the mark! The war within the mother's
> Spirit perseveres within the child.
> She can't be made amenable to rules.
> Her mother lets the elf be sway'd, not
> By decree, but by her own impulsive fancy.
> What good to her is frown or stern rebuke?
> Nay, frequent application of the rod's
> Requir'd to champion all the childish virtues.
> In giving the child existence, law was broken,
> And all is in confusion and turmoil.
> Where chaos reigns, there walks the devil.

ABIGAIL
> When I chanc'd upon the child, I confess,
> There was a radiant circle 'round her on the
> Darksome wooded-floor.

SARAH (*catching the fever*)
> > Aye, 'tis so.
> The little baggage harbors witchcraft deep
> In her. She needs no broom to fly withal.

ABIGAIL
> The scarlet letter is not made of earthly
> Cloth, but burns red-hot with fiendish fire.
> It can be seen aglow by night as Satan's
> Ward charts blacken'd wood and raven copse.

ELIZABETH
>Our very souls are now in jeopardy
>As is the name of our good colony.
>Obscenity must see the light of day
>And Hester Prynne must yet be made to pay.

ALL (*in a diminuendoing whisper*)
>Hester Prynne. Hester Prynne.

*The lights fade to tableaux on the women. Pearl sleeps in her bed.
It is late. Not far off sits Hester, who has dozed as she works her
embroidery by candlelight.*)

ELIZABETH
>Hester Prynne.

HESTER (*awakening, frightened*)
>Whose there? What evil thing cries out my name?
>'Tis nothing. My imagination is affected.
>I am too much alone, as much alone
>As if I occupied another realm.
>A ghost revisiting familiar firesides
>But can no longer make itself be seen nor felt.
>I am forgotten like the unremembered dead.
>Still, I hear the whispers of those who plot
>Against me, conspiring to take away my life.
>For all, I am an object of reproach.
>When strangers look upon my scarlet letter,
>It brands itself afresh into my soul.
>Accustom'd eye as well hath its own anguish,
>The chilling stare of intimate intolerable.
>Yet outward guise of purity is but
>A lie. If truth were known a scarlet letter
>Sears many a bosom besides my own.
>Yea, all men are guilty of a secret sin!
>Such drops of bitterness are here distilled
>Into my heart and poison every thought.
>O Fiend, whose talisman's this fatal symbol,

HESTER (*cont'd.*)
>Wouldst thou bequeath no thing to this poor sinner?
>I am the most despicable and wretched.
>Deserving nothing less than banishment –
>Much more, the very worst of punishment.

Scene Seven

The great hall of Governor Bellingham's mansion. Hester stands before the Governor, who administers the proceedings reluctantly. Also present are the reverend ministers Wilson and Dimmesdale as well as the Leech Chillingsworth.

BELLINGHAM
>Much question hath been rais'd of late concerning
>Thee. The point's been weightily discuss'd
>Whether we, that are of chief authority,
>Do well discharge our consciences to trust
>The child's soul to one that's tripp'd and fallen
>Amid the snares of this demanding world?

HESTER
>But I – I am her mother.

BELLINGHAM.
>It might be for the child's eternal welfare
>That she be taken from out thy charge and so
>Instructed closer in earthly and heavenly truths.
>What canst thou do for her in this regard?

HESTER (*clasping hand to bosom*)
>Good sirs, I can teach what I
>Have learn'd from this.

WILSON
>   Thy badge of shame?
>It is because of that same stain upon your soul
>That we'd remove thy child to purer hands.

HESTER

> This badge hath taught me,
> It daily teaches me, the lessons whereof
> My child may wiser and better be. She
> Has had good Christian nurture as suits
> A child of her small years.

WILSON

> Upon examination, I ask'd her but
> A simple question. 'Canst thou tell me,' said I,
> 'Who made thee child?' And her reply was that
> She had not been made at all, but rather
> Pluck'd from off a bush of wild rose.

Bellingham is amused by the response.

HESTER

> She's young, yet three years old and this
> Reply but fantasy suggested by
> The hips and blossoms, which oft I gather.

WILSON

> Were she the daughter from a pious home,
> She'd hear far more about our Heavenly Father.
> The child is in the dark as to her soul,
> Its present peril and future destiny.

HESTER

> From out the rank luxuriance of passion
> Has grown a beautiful, immortal flower.
> God entrusted it into my keeping.
> She is my happiness. She is my agony.
> She keeps me here in life.

BELLINGHAM

> Good woman, the child would well be car'd for
> Far better than thou –

HESTER

>   God gave her

HESTER (*cont'd.*)
> To me! Ye shall not take her!
> I would rather die!

She turns in desperation to Dimmesdale.

> Speak thou for me. Thou was my pastor
> And know'st me better than the rest. I
> Will not lose the child! Speak to them
> For thou has sympathies the others lack.
> Thou know'st what's in my heart of hearts and what
> Are mother's rights and how much stronger are they
> When she has but her child and shame. Look
> To it, I pray. I will not lose the child!

Dimmesdale is momentarily at a loss. He involuntarily presses his hand against his chest.

DIMMESDALE
> There is much truth in what she says and in
> The feeling that so inspires her. God gave
> Her the child. And gave her, too, instinctive
> Knowledge of its requirements and nature,
> Which no other mortal can possess.
> Is there not a sacred bond between a
> Mother and her child?

BELLINGHAM.
> Make plain, I pray.

DIMMESDALE
> If we deem it otherwise, do we
> Not say the Heavenly Father, Creator of all
> Flesh, hath lightly recognized a deed
> Of sin and made of no account distinction
> Between unhallow'd lust and holy love?
> The child, born of her father's guilt and of
> Her mother's shame, hath come from God to work
> In some mysterious way upon the heart,

DIMMESDALE (*cont'd.*)
>Which pleads so earnestly the right to keep her.
>The child is meant as retribution and a blessing,
>A symbol for us in the midst of troubled joy.
>She understands the solemn miracle God
>Hath wrought. This boon intends to keep her soul
>Alive and save her from the blacker depths
>Of sin which Satan sought to plunge her in.

BELLINGHAM
>Well said, good Master Dimmesdale. Well said.

A terribly shaken Dimmesdale withdraws to the side.

CHILLINGSWORTH (*more to himself*)
>He speaks, me thinks, with curious devotion.

BELLINGHAM
>And there is weighty import in all he says.
>What think you, Master Wilson? Hath he
>Not pleaded well the case of this poor woman?

WILSON.
>Indeed he hath.

BELLINGHAM (*relieved*)
>And hath adduced such arguments
>That I will leave the matter as it now stands.
>So long as there shall be no further scandal.

WILSON
>Care must be had to put the child to due
>Examination in her catechism.

BELLINGHAM
>Yes, Yes. Moreover, at the proper term, the tithing
>Men must heed the child go both to school
>And there from to our daily prayer meeting.

HESTER.
>All shall be done as you have here ordained.

BELLINGHAM.
> Good. This hapless matter's now concluded,
> And mother may with child be reunited.
> You'll find her with my sister Mistress Hibbins,
> Who, doubtless, mesmerizes her with ancient
> Tales and tutors her in garden flora.
> I bid you well, Mistress Prynne.

Pause.

> > > > > > > Why do
> You hesitate? What more assurance do you
> Need?

HESTER.
> > > None your honor. Only –

BELLINGHAM.
> > > > > > > Speak up.

HESTER.
> The gloves you placed into my care, thinking
> They were the cause of summoning here –

BELLINGHAM (*with childish enthusiasm*)
> Are they completed yet so soon? Let's see.

Hester retrieves the gloves from her basket and hands them to Bellingham.

> Fine work, indeed, you have done well.
> The delicate labor of your needle expresses
> Itself most admirably.

HESTER.
> > > > > So please, your grace.

BELLINGHAM.
> Come, I shall reward thee for thy pains.

Bellingham leads Hester off. Pause.

CHILLINGSWORTH
It's easy to see the mother's part in the child.
Would it be beyond a philosopher's extent
To analyze the child's nature and from its make
And mould give guess as to the father?

DIMMESDALE (*vehemently*)
It would be blasphemy and sin
To chase the clue with lewd philosophy! [1]
Better we should fast and pray.

WILSON (*approaching Dimmesdale*)
Still better to leave the mystery as 'tis,
'Less Providence reveals it on its own.
Thereby, every Christian man hath claim
To a father's kindness towards the hapless child.

DIMMESDALE (*to Wilson*)
In all his queries into the human frame,
It may well be, the higher faculties
Materialize, but that amid the intricacies
Of that most wondrous mechanism,
He's lost the spiritual view of life.

WILSON
                                        Lest ye
Forget, the Doctor's prov'd the concord of
Reverential and paternal love
In caring for his youthful patient.

DIMMESDALE
                        Still, his vow's
An earthly one where ours is heaven sent.

---

[1] Philosophy is used here in the 17th Century sense, meaning "science." Those who pursued natural philosophy, therefore, prescribed to logic and not to faith.

WILSON

> Be not so mindful of heaven that you
> Become no earthly good. I fear the likelihood
> Your dawning light might be extinguish'd.
> Your form grows more emaciated; your voice,
> Though rich and sweet, is prophecy of doom.

DIMMESDALE.

> I need no medicine!

Dimmesdale crosses away from Wilson.

WILSON

> How can you so contend, when every Sabbath
> Your cheek grows pale and thin? Are you so weary
> Of your employ? Or do you wish to die?

DIMMESDALE

> Were it God's will, I could be content
> My toils and grief, my sins and pains should shortly
> End with me. And what is earthly of them
> Be buri'd forever in my poor grave and that
> The spiritual go with me to my eternal
> State rather than he should exercise
> His manifold skills to proof in my behalf.

CHILLINGSWORTH

> 'Tis thus a young clergy's apt to speak.
> Youth not having taken deep root gives up
> Its hold on life so easily. The saintly man,
> Who walks with God on earth, would fain be fast
> Away to walk with him in New Jerusalem.

DIMMESDALE

> Nay, if I were worthier to walk there,
> I could be better content to toil here.

CHILLINGSWORTH

> Good men ever interpret themselves too meanly.

Chillingsworth urges Wilson to join him and speaks quietly and ardently. Dimmesdale sits apart.

CHILLINGSWORTH (*cont'd.*)
    He's entered in a desp'rate state. His malady
    Consuming him. We must act now.
    Stand firm, I pray; uphold my cause.
    I fear his life hangs in the balance.

Wilson assents. They cross to Dimmesdale.

    We'd hop'd you might select a woman from one
    Among your flock to care and ease your burdens.
    Yet, as you reject all like proposals – as if
    A priestly abstinence were law within
    Our church – we find there's no alternative.
    It is our wish, our deepest wish, that we
    Effect arrangement by which the two of us
    Were lodged as one together. Thus, it be
    That every ebb and flow of your life-tide
    Might pass the eye of this attach'd physician.

DIMMESDALE
    I am amazed, sir –

WILSON (*quickly intervening*)
                    Young reverend, restrain thyself!
    The hand of Providence has render'd this
    In purpose, sought by many personal
    And public prayers des'ring restoration
    Of our poor minister to previous health.
    Before thou speaks, remember it is a sin
    To spurn the aid which Providence extends.

Dimmesdale resigns himself as the lights cross fade.

Scene Eight

The "Witch" Mistress Hibbins, along with her companion, a woman of dark complexion, and Pearl are in the garden of the Governor's Mansion. Hester enters and Pearl runs to her. Hester picks her up and clutches her tightly.

HESTER
> Oh, my Pearl. My dear, sweet Pearl!
> I ne'er imagin'd thy embrace could feel
> More welcome than your first hour on earth.

HIBBINS (*conspiratorially*)
> Wilt thou, good Mistress, come with us tonight?
> There will be merry making in the wood,
> And I well nigh have promis'd the Dark Man,
> Comely Hester Prynne should now make one.

HESTER
> Had your brother, the governor, and other men
> Been so dispos'd to take my Pearl away,
> Gladly would I go with thee this night
> And sign my name upon the Dark Man's book
> With my own blood. But I have once
> Again receiv'd deliverance and see
> More clearly now the path which I must follow.
> Make my excuse to him, so please you Mistress.
> I stay at home this night and nights to come
> To guard safe my child, my dearest one.

Hester exits.

HIBBINS (*calling after her*)
> We'll have thee with us in the wood 'ere long,
> Mistress Prynne. We'll have thee there anon!

She laughs as the lights fade.

Scene Nine

Music: a funeral hymn. Elizabeth's house. Upstage, the deceased Elizabeth lies instate. The townswomen light candles beside her body before crossing away to prepare the wake. Hester dresses the deceased in an embroidered funeral robe and bonnet. The Chorus enters, accompanied by Pearl, now a young girl of seven.

CHORUS
       Love and hatred are both alike in passion.
       Supposing knowledge and intimacy of heart,
       They render each dependent for affection's food,
       Save that one is seen in stellar radiance,
       The other held in dark degeneracy.
       Yet by nature we humans love more than hate.
       Except where selfishness is fast at play,
       'Nless impeded by the first hostility,
       Hatred slowly transforms itself to love.
       Thus, Hester Prynne ne'er battl'd the public.
       She made no claim on it for what she suffer'd,
       Nor did she weigh upon its sympathies.
       With neither hope nor wish of gaining any thing,
       The blameless purity of her behavior
       These narrow years are reckon'd in her favor.

The Chorus sends Pearl to sit by her mother and then exits.

ABIGAIL.
       She never puts forward even the humblest title
       To share the world's privileges further than
       To breathe the common air or earn the daily
       Bread but for herself and for her child.

SARAH
       There are none so ready to give of their
       Small substance to the demand of poverty, though she
       May still alone receive the bitter gibe
       As false requital for the food she brings.

ABIGAIL

>Sure she will never hear harsh word again
>From our departed 'Lizabeth.

Abigail and Sarah snicker.

MARTHA.

>Good wives, a little thought
>Before you speak protects your sentiments
>Against the feckless winds of change. Not long
>Ago, if memory serves, one was your dearest
>Sister, the other your darkest enemy.

ABIGAIL

>Have you now changed your mind? You were from first
>Inclin'd on her behalf and oft instructed us.

MARTHA

>Hester's genuine regard for virtue has
>Indeed brought back the wand'rer to its path.
>This coming home well glads my heart and
>Justifies belief in all redemption.
>None 'mongst our circle, save Elizabeth,
>Remained hardhearted, and now as time recasts
>All things, she meets her Lord in raiment
>Fashioned by the hands of her antagonist,
>That could have well embroider'd robes of that
>Same virgin queen whose name she bore.
>Hush now. Here she comes. Speak of this no more.

Hester enters with Pearl.

HESTER

>All's done as was instructed.

MARTHA

>   And so, our thanks.
>Thy labors pass not unobserved. You are
>Welcome to stay.

HESTER
>   I have already extended
> Respects as this occasion would seem to merit.

ABIGAIL
> Our dear young minister will shortly come
> And hearten us with words of inspiration.

SARAH
> Accompanied by that Chillingsworth no doubt.

HESTER
> The hour grows late, and I must think of the child.

Hester begins to help Pearl with her cape and bonnet.

ABIGAIL (*to Sarah*)
> Why do you grudge the amity that's grown
> Between the two?

SARAH
>   It seems a thing unnatural.

ABIGAIL
> What is 'unnatural' in the sharing of two
> Cultivated minds? So few have wide
> A field the whole of human thought and study,
> Debating subjects such as faith and ethics,
> As public guise and private character.

SARAH
> He trucks with savages and magnifies
> His medical exploits by joining their
> 'Cantations. His cures, although miraculous,
> Stem from the blackest arts. And even you
> Must well admit that our sweet minister
> Grows weak and wan with every passing moon.
> Moreover, this Leech's aspect, since first he dwelt
> In town, has vastly been transfigured.
> There's something ugly in his face, nay,
> Even evil.

ABIGAIL
>   That he does not possess
> The angel face of our dear reverend
> In no way justifies your prejudice.

SARAH
> If I no better knew, I'd call him Satan's
> Emissary. He burrows in the pastor's
> Privacy and gnaws the kernel of his soul.

MARTHA
> Should there be any truth in what you say,
> I have no doubt that our brave minister
> Will exit forth from out this fray transformed
> By the glory of his deliverance.

SARAH (*near tears*)
> It saddens me to think upon the mortal
> Agony through which he toils t'wards triumph.
> And from the gloom within his eyes, I judge
> The victory's by no account assur'd.

ABIGAIL
> And what think'st Hester Prynne of this?

HESTER
> I cannot say, as neither man comes oft
> Within my sphere. But this I know, that if
> The town sees only with its eyes, it is
> Exceedingly inclined to be deceived.
> However, if judgement's formed, as I am wont
> To do, on a warm heart's intuition,
> Conclusions are profound and unmistaken.
> Now, as night advances, we must be going.

Hester exits with Pearl.

MARTHA.
> Sisters, mark her words; she counsels well.
> Would more hearts and minds were so compell'd.

Scene Ten

Dimmesdale and Chillingsworth are above on the balcony.

CHILLINGSWORTH
    Sometimes the zeal of Puritans can carry
    Narrowness so satisfied with self
    And so intractable, it starves the very
    World it's meant to feed.

DIMMESDALE
                    Such thoughts are heresy.

CHILLINGSWORTH
    Is ours a time whose only name for thought
    Is heresy? But I forget that you
    Are first a priest, a true religionist
    With reverential sentiment developed
    With order'd mind, impelling you along
    The track of creed. It is imperative
    To your assurity to feel your Faith's
    Constraint supporting you, yet blind to see
    Within its iron clasp you are confined.

DIMMESDALE
    I find occasional relief in seeing
    The universe through another's intellect,
    As with this window opened here to let
    A fresher air into this cloistered study.

CHILLINGSWORTH
    And yet your practices are more and more
    Aligned with the old, corrupted faith of Rome
    Than with the better light in which you have
    Been bred.

DIMMESDALE.
            It is my custom, as with many
    Pious Puritans, to fast and purify

DIMMESDALE (*cont'd.*)
> The body, thus rend'ring it a fitter medium
> Of heavenly illumination.

CHILLINGSWORTH
> I fear you do so far too rigorously.
> Still you keep a vigil night by night
> Until your knees beneath you tremble, as if
> It were an act of absolute remorse.
> Truly, sir, I fear for your well being.
> Does wish to be but shadow of yourself
> Evince a hope of leaving our existence?

They are interrupted by Hester and Pearl's entrance below. Hester looks up at the minister and doctor in the window.

PEARL (*tugging at her mother's arm*)
> Come away, mother. Come, or yonder
> Dark Man will capture you. He hath got hold
> Of the minister but cannot catch this Pearl.

Pearl and Hester exit.

CHILLINGSWORTH
> There is no law, nor any reverence
> For government in that poor child's
> Composition. The other day, I saw her splash
> None less than Gov'nor Bellingham
> Himself with water at the cattle trough.
> What in Heaven's name is she, this imp?
> Is she evil? Hath she herself affections?
> They say she is incapable of tears.
> What is the principle of her existence?

DIMMESDALE
> None. None, save the freedom of a broken law.
> It is as if she has been made afresh,
> From out new elements and must perforce

DIMMESDALE (*cont'd.*)
>Be authoriz'd to live her own good life.
>She is a law unto herself, and whether
>Capable of good, I cannot say.

CHILLINGSWORTH
>And with her goes a woman, who by demerits
>Hath no mystery of hidden sinfulness.
>Is Hester Prynne less miserable, think you,
>For that emblazon'd badge upon her breast?

DIMMESDALE
>I do believe it so. There was a look
>Of pain from which I'd gladly have been spar'd.
>Still, it must be better for the sufferer
>To show the pain, as that poor woman does,
>Than to imprison it within the heart.

Dimmesdale withdraws below.

CHILLINGSWORTH (*to himself*)
>Let men tremble who win a woman's hand,
>Unless they win the passion of her heart.
>Else it will be their sorry fortune when
>Some mightier touch than their own fires
>The embers of her unconscious desires.

The lights fade.

Scene Eleven

Dimmesdale, alone, splashes his face with water. He stares intently into the mirror. His father and mother appear behind a scrim.

DIMMESDALE
>Who's here? What have these spectral thoughts
>Made ghastly substance? Why father, with beard

DIMMESDALE (*cont'd.*)
>Grown white, and mother, too, with saint-like frown,
>Why do you turn your gaze away from me?
>Might not you throw a pitying glance toward your
>Tormented son? These visions delude me not.
>You are not firm in nature, not like the wall
>Or floor. Yet you are far more true, for I
>Perceive the real existence on this earth
>But through the anguish of my soul.

Chillingsworth enters. The lights cross fade as Dimmesdale hauls himself back to reality. The doctor removes plants from his basket, setting them on the desk.

DIMMESDALE
>Where pray, good doctor, did you collect
>Those herbs with such a dark and fleshy leaf?

CHILLINGSWORTH
>Near at hand, in our own cemetery.
>They're new to me. I found them on a grave
>Which bore no stone, nor any memorial
>Of deceased save these strange weeds that take
>Upon themselves to keep him in remembrance.
>Perhaps they emanate from forth his heart
>And represent some secret therein buried.

DIMMESDALE
>Good sir, that is but fantasy.

CHILLINGSWORTH (*not pointedly*)
>He had done better to confess it while in life.

DIMMESDALE (*trying to disengage*)
>Perchance, he longed to but could not.

CHILLINGSWORTH
>Could not? Wherefore could not? As all
>The powers of Nature direct confession of sin,
>So these black weeds spring forth to manifest it.

42

DIMMESDALE

>No power, save Divine Mercy, can divulge
>The secrets buri'd in the human heart.
>And that heart, making itself guilty of such
>Secrets, must garner them until that day
>When all shall be reveal'd. Nor have I read
>In Holy Writ that such disclosure's intended
>As part of retribution. Surely that were
>A shallow view of it. But this I know,
>On judgement day, that heart will yield it secrets,
>Not with reluctance, but joy unutterable.

CHILLINGSWORTH

>Then why not herald them aloud? Why not permit
>The guilty sooner profit from this solace?

DIMMESDALE

>They do. Many a soul has given confidence
>To me, not just upon their deathbed but while
>Robust in life and fair in reputation.
>And always, succeeding from that outpouring,
>What relief I've witnessed in those brethren.

CHILLINGSWORTH

>How can it be otherwise?

DIMMESDALE

>   Indeed.
>How can a wretched man, guilty, let's say,
>Of murder, prefer to keep the dead remains
>Buri'd within his heart, rather than fling
>It forth, and let the universe absolve it?

CHILLINGSWORTH

>Yet still, some men bury their secrets thus.

DIMMESDALE

>They keep a silence by the very construct
>Of their nature. Or can we not suppose that while

DIMMESDALE (*cont'd.*)
Retaining zeal for God's glory and man's
Welfare, they shrink from showing themselves black
And filthy in the opinion of fellow men.
Thus, no good can be achiev'd by them,
No evil be redeem'd by better service.
Their life an unimaginable torment.

CHILLINGSWORTH
These men deceive themselves. They fear to own
The shame that rightfully belongs to them.
If they seek to glorify Our Father,
Let them lift their unclean hands to heaven.
If they'd serve their fellow man, let them
Manifest their conscience and constrain
Their bent for penitential self-abasement.
Wouldst thou have me think, old friend, false
Show is better – can be for 'God's glory
Or man's welfare' – better than God's own truth?
Trust me, I say such men deceive themselves.

DIMMESDALE
It may be so. But, now, another matter.
I'd ask my well-skill'd physician whether,
In good sooth, he deems me to have profited
By his good care? Speak frankly.

CHILLINGSWORTH
                                        Then, freely,
The ailment is a strange one. Looking daily
At you for years gone by, I deem you are
A man sore sick.

Dimmesdale laughs.

                              Not so sick but that
A train'd and watchful physician well might
Expect to cure the malady. The disease
Is what I seem to know, yet know it not.

DIMMESDALE
>Come, you speak in riddles, learned sir.

CHILLINGSWORTH.
>Then, to speak more plainly, let me ask –
>As trusted friend – hath all the operation
>Of this disorder been honestly recounted?

DIMMESDALE
>How can you question it? 'Twere child's play
>To bid a doctor come and hide the sore.

CHILLINGSWORTH
>You'd have it, then, that I know all? A bodily
>Disease, look'd on as whole, reflects
>An ailment in the spiritual domain. Pardon,
>If my plain speech give shadow of offense,
>You, sir, of all the men whom I have known,
>Your body is conjoined the closest with
>The spirit whereof it is the instrument.

DIMMESDALE (*rising*)
>Then I need not inquire further as you
>Deal not in medicine of the soul.

CHILLINGSWORTH (*pressing*)
>A sickness in your spirit manifests
>Itself upon your body. Would you, therefore,
>Deny physician heal the bod'ly evil?
>How may this be unless you first expose
>The cancer of your soul.

DIMMESDALE
>   No!
>No, not to thee, nor any earthly physician!
>If it be the soul's disease, then I
>Commit myself to Him, the one Physician
>Of the soul. Who art thou, that meddlest
>In this matter? Who dares inject himself

DIMMESDALE (*cont'd.*)
>Between the sufferer and his God?!
>If it be his wish to cure or kill,
>Then let him do with me as must he will!

Dimmesdale furiously storms out of the room.

CHILLINGSWORTH (*recovering*)
>It is as well to have provoked this step.
>Nothing is lost. We shall be intimates again.
>O, how passion overwhelms
>This man and spirals him outside himself.
>And as with one emotion, so be it with another.
>He hath done a reckless thing for his part,
>This pious priest, in the passion of the heart.

The lights fade to black.

Scene Twelve

Dimmesdale stands in a pool of light. He speaks as if addressing his congregation from the pulpit.

DIMMESDALE.
>What good is a life of outward show
>If built upon a base wanting weight?
>All things are void of value unless they have
>Divine essence within their life's blood.
>Therefore, what am I? Of any substance?
>Or just the dim reflection of a shadow?

He begins to unfasten his garments and disrobe. A deep drone begins.

>I, whom you behold in priestly garments;
>I, who mount the sacred pulpit and turn
>My face to Heaven; I who take upon
>Myself to officiate communion;
>I, who've laid the hand of baptism on

DIMMESDALE (*cont'd.*)
>Your children; I, who've breath'd the final prayer
>For your departing friends; I, your pastor,
>The godly youth, the saint on earth, whom you
>So reverence, am utterly pollution –
>A thing of unimagined evil.
>The worst of sinners, the vilest among the vile.

Turning upstage, he tears off his shirt and raises his arms in supplication as he kneels. An enormous cross irradiates within the wooden wall.

>I, WHO WORSHIP TRUTH AND HATE THE LIE
>ABOMINATE MY SELF AND PRAY TO DIE!

He flagellates himself brutally with a bloodied scourge about his already bruised shoulders and back. On each stroke a riveting sound crescendoes. The drone becomes deafening. The lights pop to full blackness.

End of Act One

ACT TWO

Scene One

The market square. The old pillory stands center as in Act One, the great wall now split and angled as if the pillory stood at the end of a street. It is the "dark grey of midnight." Dimmesdale enters, "walking in the shadow of a dream." He slowly makes his way toward the scaffold and mounts the steps.

DIMMESDALE
It is a mockery of penitence,
A mockery at which the angels blush
And weep, while fiends rejoice with jeering laughter.
What right's infirmity like mine to burden
Itself in false remorse? I am a coward!

His turmoil erupts in a cry of pain, and he presses his chest.

'Tis done. The town will wake and hurry forth
And find me here.

Pause. Dimmesdale laughs.

But no. No one awakes.
No one stirs save these solemn phantoms
Of my thoughts. The drowsy slumberers mistook
The cry for something frightful in a dream
Or for the shriek of Mistress Hibbins as she
Rides with Satan through the air. What's this?
A glint of light approaching up the street.
Within its 'radiated orb steals forth
A figure within whose steps I hear the doom
Of my existence.

He shrinks into the shadows behind the pillory.

No, it is
The good old minister, come freshly from

DIMMSDALE (*cont'd.*)
>The side of some expiring man no doubt.
>How saint-like is his personage illum'd
>By halo radiant. It glorifies
>Amid this gloomy night of sin as if
>He had absorb'd the distant glow of that
>Celestial City, while witnessing the joyous
>Pilgrim pass within its golden gates.

John Wilson enters carrying a small lantern and crosses the stage unaware of Dimmesdale. Wilson stops, draws his coat closed against the chill of the night, and then exits. Dimmesdale cautiously steps forward and play acts.

>Good evening to you most venerable Father.
>Pray ye, come up and pass a pleasant hour
>Or two with your dear brother clergyman
>And valued friend upon this guilty scaffold.

He laughs, and his laughter is joined by another's, which is light and airy. Dimmesdale cries out.

>Pearl? Little Pearl? Hester, are you
>there?

Hester and Pearl emerge from behind the scaffold platform.

HESTER
>Yes, it is I, Hester Prynne.

DIMMESDALE
>Whence come you? What sent you hither?

HESTER
>I go to Master Winthrop's deathbed and there
>Must take his measure for a burial gown.

DIMMESDALE
>Come up hither. Ye have been here before,
>But I was not with you. Come up, and we

DIMMSDALE (*cont'd.*)
> Will stand at last all three together.

Hester and Pearl ascend the steps. Dimmesdale takes Pearl's hand as the little girl stands between her parents.

PEARL
> Minister?

DIMMESDALE
> What wouldst thou, child?

PEARL
> Wilt thou stand here
> With us tomorrow after Sabbath worship?

DIMMESDALE
> Nay. Not so, my child. But I shall stand
> With thee and with thy mother some future day.

Pearl tries to pull her hand from Dimmesdale's.

> A moment longer, child.

PEARL
> What future day?

DIMMESDALE (*whispering*)
> At judgement day. Then and there we three
> Shall stand, but light of day shall never see
> Our meeting.

Pearl tears herself away and descends the pillory. There is a flash of light, and the sky and clouds flare red as a meteor falls to earth. Pearl squeals with delight at the display. Dimmesdale presses his chest. Hester joins Pearl.

> What light shines forth, its glow so strong,
> The great vault of heaven brightens thus?
> What elements are these that fall to earth
> And color the familiar with supernatural?

The red glow fades as Pearl points at a figure across the stage.

DIMMESDALE (*cont'd.*)
    What is that man, Hester?

PEARL
    I can tell thee what he is.

DIMMESDALE
              Quickly.

PEARL
    Yonder is the Dark Man of the Wood.

DIMMESDALE
    Dost thou mock me child?

PEARL (*withdrawing*)
    Thou wouldst not promise to take my hand.

Chillingsworth emerges from the shadows and crosses to the pillory.

CHILLINGSWORTH
    Master Dimmesdale? Worthy, sir, can this
    Be you? Well, well, indeed. We men of study,
    Whose heads are in our books, we dream in waking
    Moments and walk in sleeping hours.
    Truly, have we the need to be looked after.
    Come, I pray, let me lead you home.

DIMMESDALE
    How knewest I was here?

CHILLINGSWORTH
    In good faith, I did not.
    I've spent the whole of this sad night at Master
    Winthrop's bedside, doing what my humble
    Skills allow to bring the man some ease.
    He having ventured home to a better world,
    I was likewise homeward bound, when this

CHILLINGSWORTH (*cont'd.*)
> Strange light shone forth as some presentiment
> For the weary traveler.

DIMMESDALE
> Is our destiny
> Reveal'd in hieroglyphs upon the cope of heaven?

CHILLINGSWORTH
> A scroll so wide might not be too expansive
> For Providence to write a person's fate thereon.
> Did you not see the crimson letter in the sky?
> The letter 'A.' Which I interpret stands
> For 'Angel.' As our good Master Winthrop was made
> An angel this night, it was, without a doubt,
> Deemed right that there should be some show of it.
> But come with me, good sir. I beseech you,
> Let not the chill of this dank night creep in
> Your frame and, thus, defraud your audience
> Tomorrow's prayer and holy lesson. You must
> Be fit to do your Sabbath duty.

DIMMESDALE
> I shall go with thee.

He allows himself to be led down and taken away by Chillingsworth.

CHILLINGSWORTH (*exiting*)
> You must study less and give yourself
> A little pastime, or these nightly whimsies
> Will, I fear, severely multiply.

HESTER (*stepping forth*)
> He is Satan's peddler and retails his wares
> At homes and churches, at our market squares.
> Surely my silence has proved the worst of deeds
> And Arthur must from this devil's hands be freed.

She hurries off with Pearl as the lights fade to black.

Scene Two

Chillingsworth assists the exhausted Dimmesdale onto his bed, where he collapses and almost immediately falls to sleep. Chillingsworth brushes the hair off the minister's face, and then lays his hand upon the minister's chest.

CHILLINGSWORTH (*not unsympathetically*)
Thy pale cheek's flush'd, and thy bosom burns.
Even in thy sleep the angels bring no peace.
So fair of face and form, thou art as well
Endowed from God with attributes the envy
Of us all.

Dimmesdale moans and stirs, but does not awake. Chillingsworth rises and crouches at the foot of the bed.

But beauty absolute belongs
To angels not to man, and heavenly face
And form are never match'd by purity
Of heart and soul. As pure as the multitude
Believes you, all spiritual as you appear,
With aspirations for our race's good,
With love of souls, pure sentiments, such piety,

Rising and crossing upstage, hovers over the bed.

Yet, I divine you have inherited
A strong and feral nature not exposed,
And I must excavate still further
In the direction of this precious vein to find
The truth and satisfy the craving of my mind.

Chillingsworth again lays his hand upon Dimmesdale's chest, then pulls aside the minister's vestment, exposing the minister's naked chest. Dimmesdale moans. Chillingsworth turns away with a look of horror and wonder, then rises and throws up his arms in rapture as the lights quickly fade to blackout.

Scene Three

A seagull cries. The sound of waves pummeling the shore. The lights come up to reveal Chillingsworth, with basket and staff, foraging for roots and herbs. Hester and Pearl enter.

HESTER
> I must talk with yonder gatherer of herbs.
> Run down to the margin of the sea and play
> You there with shells and tangled weed.
> Go not beyond the point from out my sight;
> I'll not be long and come to join you soon.

Pearl runs off to play, and Hester crosses to Chillingsworth.

> I would speak a word with you. A word
> Concerns us much.

CHILLINGSWORTH
>   And is it Mistress Prynne
> Who now long last has word for poor old
> Chillingsworth? Ah, with all my heart!

He rises stiffly from his knees.

> I hear good tidings of you on all accounts.
> Just yesterday, our governor divulged
> To me the Council argues whether or not,
> With safety to the common weal, the scarlet
> Letter might be remov'd from off your bosom.
> On my life, I made entreaty unto him
> That such discharge might be enacted straightaway.

HESTER
> Removal lies not within the Council's pleasure.
> Were I so worthy to be rid of it, by its
> Design the badge would rend and fall away.

CHILLINGSWORTH
> Nay, then wear it if it suits you better.
> A woman must needs to follow her own fancy,

CHILLINGSWORTH (*cont'd.*)
    And bravely it bares itself upon your breast.

  Pause.

    What see you in my face that causes you
    To fix your eye and stare so earnestly?

HESTER
    Something to make me weep if there were tears
    Bitter enough to shed for it.

CHILLINGSWORTH
                      The years
    Since last we spoke have wrought great change.
    I have grown old, the traces of advancing
    Life more evident in line and beard.

HESTER
    I see so little feature of the man I knew:
    An intellectual man, and gentle too,
    Who was by nature and design both calm
    And quiet. That is what I most recall of him.

CHILLINGSWORTH
    And that aspect has altogether vanish'd?

HESTER
    Succeeded by a fierce and guarded look.

  Chillingsworth smiles.

    But let it pass, I pray, for it is not
    My purpose here. It is of yonder miserable
    Man that I would speak.

CHILLINGSWORTH
                 And what of him?
    Speak freely, and I will make due answer
    And be quite heartened for the opportunity.
    Come, there is no need to hide the truth
    From him who is your only confidante.

HESTER

> When last we spoke, it was your will to wrest
> From me a pledge of secrecy as to
> The bond betwixt yourself and me. There seem'd
> No choice to me but silence, for his life
> Was in your hands. It was with grave misgivings
> That in accord with your behest, I thus
> Constrain'd myself – having cast off all duty
> Towards others, there yet remained a duty towards him.
> I realize now in pledging oath to keep
> Your charge that I most grievously betray'd him.
> Since then no man is more his intimate.
> You tread behind his every step and are
> Beside him in his wake and in his sleep.
> You probe his thoughts and burrow in his heart,
> Causing him to die each day a living death.
> And still he knows you not. In permitting this,
> I have prov'd myself most false to him.

CHILLINGSWORTH

> What choice had you? My finger pointed at the man
> And would have dragg'd him from his pious pulpit
> Toward the dungeon and thence to gallows.

HESTER

> It had been better so!

CHILLINGSWORTH

> 　　　　　　　　　　What evil have I
> Done the man? The richest fee that ever
> Monarch paid physician could not have bought
> Such care as I have wasted on your priest.
> But for my aid, his life would have been burn'd
> Away within the early years of his torment.
> Yon 'miserable' man, he lack'd your nerve and strength
> To bear the burden brought forth by scarlet letter.
> O, such goodly secrets could I reveal!

CHILLINGSWORTH (*cont'd.*)
>Enough! What art can do, I have exhausted.
>That he now breathes is owing all to me.

HESTER.
>Better he had died at once.

CHILLINGSWORTH.
>   Truly,
>Yes, better had he died at once,
>For ne'er did mortal suffer as he's suffer'd,
>And all was in the sight of his betrayer.
>O, he has been conscious of me and felt
>My influence as curse upon his heart,
>For ne'er has God devis'd so sensitive a man.
>He knew an eye examin'd him, which sought
>Revenge, but knew not the eye was mine.
>The superstition of his brotherhood,
>It fancied demons caus'd the desp'rate
>Thoughts and frightful dreams. Remorse's sting
>And pardon's despair were but a foretaste
>Of what awaits for him beyond the grave.
>Nor did he stray, but kept all well conceal'd
>From the e'er-constant shadow of my presence.
>Thus, I, whom he had vilely wrong'd,
>Surviv'd but through the poison of revenge.
>A mortal man, with once a human heart,
>For his express'd torment became a fiend.

HESTER
>Hast thou not tortur'd him enough?
>Has he not paid thee all and more?

CHILLINGSWORTH
>No. No. He has increased the debt.
>Dost thou recall me not as once I was?
>My life was true and earnest, with days devoted
>To scholarship and mankind's betterment.

CHILLINGSWORTH (*cont'd.*)
>No life had been more peaceful than my own,
>Few lives so rich with benefits conferred.
>Was I not kind and just and loyal –

HESTER
>All this and more.

CHILLINGSWORTH
>>>>And now what?
>A fiend, most evil. And who made me so!

HESTER
>It was myself, I, no less than he.
>Why hast thou not avenged thyself on me?

CHILLINGSWORTH
>Thy rebuke I've left upon the scarlet letter.
>If it has not aveng'd, I can no more.

HESTER
>It has avenged thee.

CHILLINGSWORTH
>>>>I judg'd no less.

HESTER
>It has, moreover, disciplin'd me to the truth.
>I must divulge the secret. He must discern thy
>Character, what e'er it cost. The debt
>I owe to him must at length be paid.
>The overthrow of fame and earthly state,
>Perchance, his very life, are in thy hands.
>I see no good for him to live a life
>Of emptiness. I shan't implore thy mercy.
>Do as thou wilt with him. There is no good
>For him, no good for me, no good for thee!
>There is no path to guide us from this maze.

Hester starts to leave.

CHILLINGSWORTH
> I could well pity thee. Thou hast great elements.
> Hadst thou sooner met a better love than mine,
> This evil would not have been. I pity thee
> For the good that has been wasted in thy nature.

HESTER
> And I thee for the hate that's transformed thine.
> Wilt thou yet purge it out of thee and be
> Once more human? If not for his sake, then doubly
> For thine own! Forgive and leave his further
> Retribution to the Power governing it.
> I said just now, no good can come for him
> Or thee, or me, who haunt this maze of evil,
> Stumbling o'er the guilt we cast before us.
> It is not so! There can be good for thee,
> And thee alone, since thou was deeply wrong'd
> And has it at thy will to exonerate.
> Wilt thou surrender up that privilege?
> Wilt thou reject that priceless benefit?

CHILLINGSWORTH
> Hester, it is not granted me to pardon.
> I have no power as thou attributes me.
> My creed interprets all we do and suffer.
> By thy first step awry, thou planted evil.
> And since that time, all has been necessity.
> It is our fate.

Pause.

> The black flower blossoms as it may.
> Do what thou must. Now, be on thy way.

Chillingsworth dismisses her with a wave and stoops down to continue his harvesting. Hester crosses away and looks back.

HESTER
>Why does the tender grass not sere and brown
>Beneath his steps? Why does the wholesome growth
>Not turn malignant at his very touch?
>If he should sink asudden into the earth,
>From out that barren spot would spring a gnarl
>Of most infectious bane or deadly nightshade.
>He has done me far worse than I did him.
>I hate this man though it be counted sin.

She exits as the lights fade. The sound changes from crashing waves to the call of a lone songbird.

Scene Four

Deep in the recesses of the forest. The wall is gone or tall vertical louvers throughout have opened, revealing the horizon and sky as if seen through the trunks of stately trees. Low mist and shafts of dappled sunlight bath the forest floor. Hester and Pearl enter. As they progress from pool to pool of light, the sun shies away from them.

PEARL.
>Look, mother! The sun, it loves you not.
>But runs away and hides itself. See now.

The pool of light at their feet fades as another pool nearby comes up.

>There. There it is, playing, a good way off.
>Stand you here, and let me run and catch it.
>I am a child. It will not flee from me,
>For I wear nothing yet upon my bosom.

HESTER
>Nor ever will, my child, I pray.

PEARL
>   Why not?
>Will not it come when I am grown a woman?

HESTER
Run away, my child, and catch the sun!

Pearl runs into the pool and embraces the sunlight.

PEARL
Look. Look! My hands reach out and grasp –

The sun fades, but Pearl smiles, her expression brightening as if she absorbed the light. She runs to the next pool, where the process is again repeated.

HESTER
Come sit by me and rest thyself.

PEARL
I am not tired, mother. But I will come
If thou will tell a story.

HESTER.
A story? 'Bout what?

PEARL.
About the Dark Man, who haunts the wood,
Carrying a book with him with iron clasps;
And those he meets he asks they write their names
In blood upon the pages of this book;
And then he sets his mark upon their breast.

HESTER
And who told you this tale?

PEARL
The old witch,
Mistress Hibbins. She said the scarlet letter
Was the Dark Man's mark on thee and that
It glows like flame when thou encounters him
In field or wood at dead of night.

HESTER
And didst
Thou ever wake and find thy mother gone?

PEARL

> Not that I recall, but tell me now,
> Does such a man exist? And didst thou ever
> Meet with him and sign your name within his book,
> And is this here his mark upon your breast?

HESTER (*laughing*)

> Peace, child. Peace! Thou takes away
> My breath as does the icy ocean wind.
> Wilt thou let me alone if I concede?

PEARL

> Yes, but only if thou tellest all.

HESTER

> Then, yes, just once I met this Man,
> And this, the scarlet letter, is his mark.
> Now, come, and question me no more.
> Sit here by me, and let me sing a song.

Pearl relents and sits beside her mother.

PEARL

> A song 'bout what?

HESTER

> About yon brook.
> Cans't thou not hear its murmuring?

She sings.[2]

> WHAT IF A DAY, OR A MONTH, OR A YEAR,
> CROWN THY DELIGHTS WITH A THOUSAND SWEET
> CONTENTINGS,
> A THOUSAND SWEET CONTENTINGS?
> MAY NOT CHANGE OF A NIGHT OR AN HOUR
> CROSS THY DELIGHTS WITH AS MANY SAD

---

[2] The score to "What If A Day" is found in the Appendix pp. 90-91.

HESTER (*singing cont'd.*)
>TORMENTINGS,
>AS MANY SAD TORMENTINGS?
>
>ALL IN HAZARD THAT WE HAVE,
>HERE IS NOTHING BIDING;
>DAYS OF PLEASURE ARE AS STREAMS
>THROUGH FAIR FORESTS GLIDING.
>WEAL OR WOE, TIME DOTH GO,
>TIME HATH NO RETURNING;
>SECRET FATES GUIDE OUR STATES
>BOTH IN MIRTH AND MOURNING.

PEARL
>Why is the brook so sad, mother? Tell me.

HESTER.
>If thou hadst sorrow of thine own, the brook
>Might sing of it to thee, e'en as it sings
>To me of mine.

PEARL.
>   Will Pearl have such a sorrow?

HESTER. (*quoting Proverbs*)
>'Ev'n in laughter the heart is sad, for well
>It knows that after joy comes but sorrow.'

Hester ruffles to attention having heard a noise.

>Hush now, I hear a step along the path.
>I'd have thee take thyself to play and leave
>Me here alone to speak with him who comes.

PEARL
>Is it the Dark Man?

HESTER
>   Go now and play.
>Do not stray far into the wood and heed
>Thou come to me with haste at my first call.

PEARL

> If 'tis the Dark Man, wilt thou let me stay?

HESTER

> Go, silly child! It is no Dark Man.
> Can'st thou not see him walking through the trees?
> It is the minister.

PEARL

> Ah, so it is.
> He has his hand upon his heart. Is it
> Because he wrote his name in the Dark Man's book?

HESTER

> Go now! Keep where thou hearst the brook.

> *Pearl exits singing, and Hester withdraws into the shadows. After a time, Pearl's singing fades, and then Dimmesdale enters.*

HESTER

> Arthur Dimmesdale.

DIMMESDALE

> Who speaks?

HESTER

> 'Tis I.

DIMMESDALE

> Hester?
> Hester Prynne! Is't thou? Art thou in life?

HESTER

> Even so. In such a life as has been but mine
> These many years. And thou, Arthur Dimmesdale,
> Dost thou yet live?

DIMMESDALE (*reaching out for her hand*)

> If I may trust this hand
> Be mine and thou not apparition.
> Thy grasp is cold, and yet in it I find assurance
> That we inhabit again this self same sphere.

HESTER
>Come, stay with me awhile and in
>The cover of this wood, espouse a moment's
>Armistice from the conflicts of this world.

Hester smiles and slowly leads him to a sunny spot where they sit down.

DIMMESDALE
>Hast thou, Hester, found some peace?

HESTER
>   Hast thou?

DIMMESDALE
>None. None save misery, being what I am.
>What else could I expect? Were I an atheist,
>I might have found some peace, or if a man
>Devoid of conscience, should ne'er have lost it.

HESTER
>People reverence thee for thy good work.
>Does this not bring thee consolation?

DIMMESDALE
>Only misery. More misery as I
>Have little faith in it. It is delusion.
>What can a ruin'd soul like mine effect
>Towards other souls' redemption? Better
>Reverence converts to scorn and hatred.
>Canst thou deem it a consolation that I
>Must stand upon the pulpit and meet so many
>Faces gazing up toward me as if the light
>Of heaven discharg'd from out my very lips?

HESTER
>You wrong yourself in this. You have repented.
>Your sin is left behind in days long past.
>Your present life is no less holy than it
>Seems in people's eyes. There is reality

HESTER (*cont'd.*)
>In penitence that's seal'd and witness'd by good
>Deeds. Why should they not bring you some peace?

DIMMESDALE (*rising*)
>No. There is no substance in it. It is but
>Cold and dead and can do no thing for me.
>Of penance I've had enough. Of penitence
>There has been none. Or else I would have long
>Ago cast off these garments and reveal'd
>Myself as I will stand on judgement day.
>Bless'd are you that wear the scarlet letter
>Openly for mine burns secretly within.
>Had I a friend, or were it my worst enemy,
>To whom I could each day betake myself
>And thus be known as vilest sinner, methinks
>My soul might keep itself thereby alive.
>Even this much of truth would rescue me.
>But all is falsehood, emptiness, and death.

HESTER
>Such a friend as thou has wished for, has thou
>In me, thy partner in this ignominy.

DIMMESDALE
>What relief it is to look into an eye
>That recognizes me for what I am.

HESTER
>And thou has long had such an enemy
>That dwelt with thee beneath thy roof.

DIMMESDALE
>An enemy? What do you mean? Beneath my roof?

HESTER.
>O, Arthur, forgive me! In all things else
>Have I attempted honesty. Through all
>Extremity, the virtue I embrac'd most firm

HESTER (*cont'd.*)
>Was truth. But when thy good, thy fame, thy very
>Life were put in question, then, I approv'd
>Deception. But I have learn'd, though death may threaten,
>No good can come from lies.

Pause

>Dost thou not see what I would say?
>The old man, the leech, who you call Roger
>Chillingsworth. He was my husband!

Dimmesdale freezes for a moment, then sinks to the ground.

DIMMESDALE
>I might have known. I did know.
>My heart's recoil at first espying him
>Told the secret. Why did I not attend?
>Why not perceive? O, Hester, to expose
>My sick and guilty heart to the eye that gloats
>On it. O, God, the horror of it.
>The shame! How could you lie to me?
>How could you hide such wickedness?
>How can I forgive thee?

HESTER
>Thou shalt forgive me. Thou shalt.
>The world has frown'd on me, and yet I bore it.
>Heaven likewise frown'd on me, and yet
>I did not die. But thy
>Frown is more than I can bear and live.
>Therefore, wilt thou frown upon me?
>Wilt thou not forgive thy Hester,
>The one for whom you swore eternal love?
>We are not the worst of sinners in the world.
>This man's revenge is blacker than our own;
>He desecrates the sacred human heart.
>Never did thou and I transgress as such.
>Our love had consecration of its own.

HESTER (*cont'd.*)

> We felt it so. We said so to each other.
> Hast thou forgotten? Arthur?

DIMMESDALE

> I have not.
> Forgive me, Hester, as I forgive thee.
> I who have been false to God and false
> To man, might be for one brief moment true.
> I forgive you.

HESTER (*embracing him*)

> May God forgive us both.

> *Pause*

DIMMESDALE

> Chillingsworth, he knows of your intent,
> To expose his true identity?

HESTER

> He does.

DIMMESDALE

> And think you then that he will keep our secret?

HESTER

> There is a mystery within his nature
> Grown by exercise of his revenge.
> It is not likely he'll betray the secret
> But seek elsewhere to satisfy obsession.

DIMMESDALE

> What'll be the course of his revenge?
> How am I to breathe the self-same air?
> What can I do? Think for me, Hester.

HESTER

> Thou must abide no longer with this man,
> Thy heart a mark to his predation.

DIMMESDALE

'Tis fortune
Worse than death, but what alternative
Remains to me? Must I sink deeper
Upon these wither'd leaves and die?
The hand of judgement rests upon my head.

HESTER

Heaven would show thee mercy if thou has strength
Enough to welcome it.

DIMMESDALE

Be strong for me. Advise my course.

HESTER

Is the world so narrow? Lies the universe
Within the compass of our small settlement?
Doth this wooded path lead only backward,
Never forward, into a wilderness
Free from man's o'erstepping tread, a brief
Sojourn from this a world where thou has been
Most wretched, to one where thou may'st still
find happiness?

DIMMESDALE

Such happiness is found
Beneath these fallen leaves.

HESTER

There is as well
The sea's broad path. It brought thee hither, and if
Thou choose, it can transport thee back again
To native soil, wherein some vast metropolis
Or far-off village –

DIMMESDALE

It cannot be.
I'm powerless to leave for Providence

DIMMESDALE (*cont'd.*)
>Has plac'd me here, and lost as is my soul,
>I would still do for others what I can.

HESTER
>Thou art crush'd beneath the weight of misery,
>But thou shalt leave this pain behind; it shall
>Not cumber thee along the path nor shalt
>Thou freight the ship with it, shouldst thou prefer
>To cross the open sea. Leave this wreck
>And ruin here. Meddle no more with it.
>Begin anew!

DIMMESDALE
>How can I dare to quit my post?

HESTER
>Hast thou exhausted all possibility?
>Not so! The future's full of trial
>And triumph. There's yet much good to be effected.
>Exchange this false life for one that's true.
>Be a teacher or, if the spirit summon thee,
>An apostle of the heathen native, or
>As more thy nature is, a scholar sage
>Among the wisest and renown'd of Europe.
>Preach. Write. Act. My God,
>Do any thing save lie down and die!

DIMMESDALE
>O, Hester, thou speak'st of running to a man
>Whose knees are tott'ring beneath him.

HESTER
>Give up thy name and make thyself another
>Such as thou canst with pride and dignity maintain.
>Why shouldst thou tarry yet another day
>In torments that have gnaw'd away thy life
>And made thee weak to hope, to will, to do,
>Even so powerless to find repentance?

DIMMESDALE.
>The scarlet letter's been your passport to
>Alien regions where I dare not to step.
>Your intellect and heart have found its home in desert
>Places free of human institution.
>There is no strength nor courage left in me
>To venture forth into these worlds alone.

HESTER
>Thou shalt not go alone.

DIMMESDALE (*pause*)
>If, in all these years gone past, I could
>Recall one moment's peace or hope, I might
>Endure. But since I am irrevocably
>Doom'd, wherefore should I not grasp the solace
>Granted the condemned before his execution?
>Or if this path lead on to better life,
>As you persuade, I do renounce no fairer
>Prospect by pursuing it. What more, I can
>No longer live without your company
>So powerful are you to soothe and to sustain.

HESTER
>Thou wilt go?

DIMMESDALE
>
>Yes. Yes!

They stare at each other a moment. Smile. This happiness so foreign to them that they are not sure of the emotion.

>Do I feel joy again? I thought the germ
>Of it was dead in me. O, Hester,
>Truly, thou art my sun and better angel.
>I flung myself despairingly upon
>These forest leaves, and rise again anew
>With fresh puissance to glorify Him that hath
>Shown mercy. This is already the better
>Life. Why did we not unearth it sooner?

Hester removes the scarlet letter from her bosom and tosses it aside.

HESTER

O, exquisite joy! I had not known
Its full ordeal until I felt this freedom.

She takes off her cap and her long hair falls free. From around her mouth and out of her eyes radiates a smile, gushing from the very heart of womanhood. The sun penetrates the dark canopy and lights Hester and Arthur. She raises her arms to embrace it.

Look, the sun smiles down on us,
Gladdening each leaf and limb with heavenly light.

She spins and dances in the light. She suddenly stops and speaks very rapidly.

Thou must know Pearl. Our Pearl.
Thou has observed the child, of course, I know
But thou wilt see her now with other eyes
She is a curious one. At times I must
Confess I hardly comprehend the sprite myself,
But thou wilt love her dearly, as I do
And wilt advise me how to deal with her.

DIMMESDALE

Think my acquaintance now will glad the child?

HESTER

Sure she will love thee dearly and thou her.
She's not far off. I'll call her here. Pearl!
Pearl!!

DIMMESDALE

                                    I see her there, across the brook,
Surrounded in a shaft of light.

HESTER

                                                   Thinkst thou
Her beautiful? With natural skill she's made
Those simple flowers regal ornaments.

DIMMESDALE
>If they were emeralds, diamonds, rubies red,
>They could become her little better. But –

HESTER
>What?

DIMMESDALE
>Will she truly love me?
>She's caused me much alarm, and I have long
>Recoil'd from her.

HESTER
>From Pearl? What cause hadst thou?

DIMMESDALE
>To think my features duplicated in her face
>That all the world might recognize myself.

HESTER
>Thou need'st not fear to trace whose child she is.
>See how enchanting is her beauty –
>With garlands in her hair, as if
>Some fairy-nymph of England cast a spell.
>Let her see nothing strange, no passion or misgiving.
>Our Pearl's a fitful elf, intolerant
>Of feelings she can't appreciate.

DIMMESDALE
>My heart suspects this interview, yet longs
>For it. Children are not wont to be
>Familiar with me. They do not climb upon
>My knee nor answer to my smile.

HESTER.
>She
>Hath strong attachments, but loves me well
>And will love thee.

Pearl enters and stops upon seeing Dimmesdale with Hester. She has adorned herself with anemones, columbine and sprays of greenery.

HESTER (*cont'd.*)

                          Come dearest
Child. How slow thou art.
When hast thou been so sluggish?
Here is a friend of mine, who must be thine
As well. Now thou wilt have two times the love
As singly could thy mother give thee.

Pearl stares at Dimmesdale who raises his hand to his chest. Then she fixes her stare on her mother, raises her hand and points to Hester's breast.

Strange child, why comes thou not to me?
Hasten, Pearl, or I'll be vexed with thee.

Pearl points even more emphatically, and then bursts into a fit of shrieking, gesticulating and stamping her feet.

I see what ails the child.

DIMMESDALE

                         I pray you then
If thou lov'st me, then pacify the girl.

HESTER

Pearl, look down at thy feet. Pearl there!

Hester points to the discarded scarlet letter not far from Pearl.

Bring it hither.

PEARL

                       Come thou and take it up.

HESTER

Was ever such a child? But she is right.
I must endure this hateful token awhile
Longer, until we have departed from these shores.

HESTER (*cont'd.*)
>The forest cannot conceal it, but the ocean will swallow
>It forever.

>*Hester crosses to Pearl, retrieves the scarlet letter and re-pins it to her breast.*

>Dost thou know thy mother now?
>Wilt thou come, since she assumes her shame?

PEARL
>Now, art thou my mother and I thy Pearl.

>*Pearl takes her mother's outstretched hand and pulls her head down to kiss Hester on the cheek. Then she unexpectedly kisses the scarlet letter.*

HESTER
>When thou has shown me love, why mockest me?

PEARL
>Why doth the minister stay yonder?

HESTER
>   To welcome thee.
>Come, entreat his blessing. He loves thee greatly
>As well thy mother.

PEARL
>   He loves us well?

HESTER
>   Yes.

PEARL
>And will he go with us, hand in hand,
>Into the town?

HESTER
>   Not now. But soon.
>He'll walk with us, and we will have a home
>And hearth, and thou shall sit upon his knee.

PEARL
> And will he keep his hand upon his heart?

HESTER
> Foolish child! Come and ask his blessing!

Pearl is dragged to Dimmesdale. He hesitates and then bends down and kisses her on the brow. Pearl breaks away from her mother with a small scream and runs away. She takes some of the flowers and vigorously uses them to wash away the kiss.

> Forgive her. Let not her spitefulness eclipse
> The light of our exhilaration.
> Her nature's such to bring both joy and sorrow.

DIMMESDALE
> She was not born of love, not even purpose,
> But from our lust.

HESTER
>   But in her life, our passion
> Has transformed itself to truest love
> And foreordained a world of greater promise.
> Be only firm and patient with her, and time
> Will make amends. Now, turn from this
> And glad our hearts with plans of our departure.
> I know a ship that sails this week for England;
> A merchantman for Bristol bound and captained
> By a Spaniard. He entertains himself
> A bon vivant and recent business with him
> Confirms for me we may secure our passage
> On his ship and trust in his discretion.

DIMMESDALE
> In three days hence, I am to give the Election
> Speech. Old Bellingham has been my friend
> These many years, and I have promised to bless
> This ceremony. How can I break my oath?

HESTER

> Thou must not. Thou shouldst not.
> Rather, as Governor extends farewell
> And passes the scepter of office to his successor,
> Make thy speech a valedictory.
> Let it serve as illustration of divine
> Commencement. By doing so, thou honors both
> Thy pledge and leaves a lasting legacy.

DIMMESDALE

> How feebly and with frequent pause of breath
> I've labor'd o'er this forest's rustic path.
> Yet these surroundings now devise a haunting
> Aspect, informing me that I have either
> Dream'd 'fore this or else am dreaming now.

HESTER

> Thou dost not dream. This *terra firma*. This hand
> Substantial. Take hold of it and walk with me.
> Leave behind this dour world of pain and strife.
> And let us forge together a brand new life.

Dimmesdale pauses momentarily and then joyously takes Hester's hand. The lights fade to black as they quickly exit.

Scene Five

In the market place before the great hall as in Act One. The pillory stands in the same position. Towns— and crafts folk are gathering, along with natives, sailors, etc. There is a general festive air, one of expectancy and joy. The seamen, who drink from flasks, are tolerated but given a wide birth by the abstemious Puritans. Hester enters with Pearl.

PEARL

> What is this mother? Why have all the people
> Left their work today? There is the blacksmith.
> He's washed his face and wears his Sabbath clothes.

PEARL (*cont'd.*)
    And there is Master Brackett, the jailer. Why does
    He nod at me?

HESTER

                He recalls thee as a baby.

PEARL
    He should not smile at me. No others do.
    He is an ugly-eyed old man.

HESTER (*half-amused*)

                    Hush now.
    Look about and see what wondrous faces
    Gather here among this throng. There
    A noble native long side the house and there
    A Spanish buccaneer from off his ship.

PEARL
    Why have they come here to the square?

HESTER
    They wait as we to see the promenade.
    The magistrates come from the meetinghouse
    To celebrate today's inauguration
    Of their new governor.

PEARL
    And will the minister be here?

HESTER

                    Of course,
    But he'll not greet thee here today, and thou
    Must not greet him.

PEARL

                  But why? Among
    This crowd he knows us not? Nor must we know
    Him? He is a strange unhappy man.

HESTER
>Quiet. Thou understandest not these things.
>Look and see how cheerful are the people.
>Today another governor begins
>His rule. And they rejoice as if a safe
>And prosperous time were 'bout to blanket
>Their impoverish'd world.

On the pillory, two masters of defense commence an exhibition with buckler and broadsword. Pearl looks to Hester, who nods permission, and Pearl joins their growing audience. Hester, alone, looks around at all the people. To herself.

>Look your last upon the scarlet letter.
>Awhile and I shall be beyond your reach.
>The ocean deep will quench and hide forever
>The symbol ye have sear'd into my breast.
>The wine of life, henceforth, to be presented
>To my lips will be exhilarating
>In its chas'd and golden beaker or else will leave
>A weary, inescapable languor,
>After the lees of bitterness with which
>I have been drugg'd as with a cordial
>Of intensest potency.

Chillingsworth enters in conversation with the Ship Captain. Hester watches them. The Captain leaves Chillingsworth and crosses to Hester.

CAPTAIN (*with a Spanish accent*)
>Mistress Prynne.

HESTER
>Good day, Captain.

CAPTAIN
>I must bid
>The steward make ready one more berth than you
>Have bargain'd for. No fear of scurvy or fever

CAPTAIN (*cont'd.*)
>This voyage, what with my ship's surgeon
>And now this noted doctor.

HESTER.
>What mean you?

Staring at Chillingsworth, who nods courteously to her.

CAPTAIN
>Why, know you not that this physician –
>Chillingsworth, he calls himself – is minded
>Like to try my cabin-fare with you.
>He tells me he is of your party and close as
>Friend to the gentle man of whom you spake.
>Have I mistaken –

HESTER.
>They know each other well.
>Pray, sir, excuse me. I must prepare –

Hester quickly crosses to collect Pearl. Music and drums interrupt their exit. Townswomen enter in rapture, praising Dimmesdale's speech. They are followed by the Beadle, soldiers, magistrates, etc.)

ABIGAIL
>Never has man spoken so high, so holy.
>Never has inspiration breathed so through
>Such mortal lips than it through his.

SARAH (*in a swoon*)
>My soul was born aloft. Give space, I pray.

ABIGAIL (*supporting her.*)
>He cast a spell o'er our whole fellowship,
>Converting atmosphere to words of flame.

SARAH
>His strength was not of body but of spirit.
>Imparted him by angelic ministrations.

ABIGAIL
> Divine inspiration descended upon him
> Possessing him, so that he follow'd not
> His text but spoke extemporaneous.

SARAH
> He spoke as one who'll soon depart this earth.

ABIGAIL
> It was as if an angel, in his passage heavenward
> Had shaken his bright wings o'er us –
> At once a shadow and a splendor –
> And shower'd each with golden truths.

Dimmesdale enters. He is exhausted, falters, and John Wilson comes to his side. Dimmesdale straightens and begins to greet his adoring parishioners.

MARTHA
> He spoke as an Old Testament prophet,
> Betokening our infant colony
> Is blessed beneath celestial guardianship
> And prophesying a glorious destiny.

Hester tries again to leave, but Mistress Hibbins blocks her retreat.

HIBBINS
> What mortal imagination could conceive it?
> Yonder man divine, that saint on earth
> As all the people hold him to be, couldst thou
> Tell me if he could be the very man
> Whom thou encounter'd on the forest path?

HESTER
> Mistress, I know not of what you speak.

HIBBINS
> Fie, woman. Fie! Dost thou think
> That I've not been to wood so many times
> And have no skill to judge who else

HIBBIINS (*cont'd.*)
Has trod upon that path? I know thee,
Hester Prynne, for I behold thy token.
But what is it the minister seeks to hide
With hand plac'd so upon his heart?

PEARL
What, Mistress Hibbins? Hast thou seen it?

HESTER (*brusquely*)
It's not for us to speak like this of our
Dear minister.

HIBBINS (*to Pearl*)
No matter.
Thou wilt see soon enough.
They say thou issues from the Prince of Air.
Wilt thou ride with me some night and seek
Thy father?

Hibbins laughs shrilly, so all can hear. Along with the others, Dimmesdale turns towards Hester and Pearl who stand at the other side of the stage. Hibbins laughs loudly and withdraws pointing at Dimmesdale for all to see.

Then thou shalt know
Wherefore he keeps his hand upon his heart.

Dimmesdale is transfixed. He senses Chillingsworth nearby. The minister, the life force draining from his body, falters. Wilson comes to his side but is rebuffed. Pause. Slowly, Dimmesdale stretches out his arms.

DIMMESDALE
Hester. Come hither. Come, my little Pearl.

CHILLINGSWORTH (*rushing to Dimmesdale*)
Hold! Are you mad! What is your purpose?
Wave back the child. Cast off the woman. Do not
Bring infamy upon your office, nor blacken

CHILLINGSWORTH (*cont'd.*)
>Fame, and thereby perish in dishonor,
>All shall be well. I can yet save you.

DIMMESDALE
>Save me? Ha! Tempter, thou are too late.
>With God's help, I shall escape thy power.

Hester has once again started to lead Pearl offstage. Again, Dimmesdale extends his arms to her.

>In the name of Him who gives me grace at this
>Last moment, to do what I withheld so long,
>Come hither now and twine thy strength 'round me.
>Guided by the will which God has granted me,
>Oppose this wretched man with all thy might.

Pause

>Hester, come. Help me...to the scaffold.

The crowd remains silent. Hester is greatly conflicted, fearing the consequences of her decision. Finally, she relinquishes and crosses to Dimmesdale. He leans upon her and takes Pearl's hand as they support him toward the scaffold. Chillingsworth follows them.

CHILLINGSWORTH
>Hadst thou searched the whole earth over
>There was no place so high, so low, so secret
>Where thou couldst have escaped me save
>That scaffold.

DIMMESDALE.
>Thanks be to Him, who's led me hither.

To Hester

>Is this not better than what we dreamed?

D. A. Dorwart

HESTER

>I know not. Better? Yea,
>So we may die and Pearl along with us!

They mount the scaffold.

DIMMESDALE

>For thee and Pearl, be it as God shall order.
>He is most merciful. Let me now do
>His will. Let me make haste and take my shame
>Upon me. For Hester, I am a dying man.

Hester and Pearl help Dimmesdale face the crowd. He straightens and stands alone.

>People of this New England. Ye that lov'd me,
>Ye that deem'd me holy. Behold me now,
>The one true sinner of the world.
>At last, I stand upon the spot where seven
>Years ago I should have stood beside
>This woman, whose strength and will sustain me.
>Beside this woman, who wears the scarlet letter
>And who, where e'er she walked, was made the victim
>Of your disdain and vile hatred, there stands
>One whose brand of sin was even worse.
>God's eye beheld it. The Angels aim'd at it.
>The Devil touch'd it with his scorching hand.
>Throughout, he hid it cunningly and walk'd
>Amongst you, a mournful spirit, so pure in sin
>And e'en bereft of heavenly kindred.
>Now he stands before you and bids you look
>Once more upon this woman's scarlet letter.
>He tells you it is but the shadow of what
>He bears upon his breast. Stand any here
>Who question God's judgement on the sinner?
>Then behold the dreadful witness of it.
>Behold God's judgement!

He tears away his ministerial band and reveals his thin, pale breast upon which is centered a flush, perhaps abraded from rubbing and pressing. It is only vaguely of triangular shape. There are, however, bruises and sores about the chest and shoulders. He stands momentarily in the glow of triumph and then sinks to the floor. Hester cradles him.)

CHILLINGSWORTH
>Thou hast escaped me.

DIMMESDALE (*to Chillingsworth*)
>May God forgive thee.

He turns to Pearl.

>My little Pearl, my precious child. Wilt thou
>Kiss me now?

Pearl hesitates and then kneels down and kisses his lips, her tears dropping on his cheek. Dimmesdale smiles.

>Thou weeps, my child. She weeps!
>And with her tears, the spell is broken.
>Her mission is at last fulfilled.
>Farewell Hester.

HESTER
>Shall we not meet again?
>Shall we not spend immortal life together?
>Surely we have ransom'd one another with this woe.
>Tell me it is so.
>Thou lookest yet into eternity.
>What seest thou there? Tell me!

DIMMESDALE
>Peace, Hester. Peace. I pray.
>When we forgot our God and violated
>Reverence for one 'nother's soul,
>'Twas vain to hope that we could meet again
>In lasting union. God has prov'd his mercy,

DIMMESDALE (*cont'd.*)
> Through my afflictions, by sending us yonder
> Dark man and bringing me here before
> The people to die a death of triumphant shame.
> His will be done. Farewell. Prais'd be his name.

Dimmesdale dies. Hester and the townswomen weep. A boy soprano begins singing a hymn softly.[3] As if pained by the music, Chillingsworth withdraws to the side of the stage a broken man. A townswoman adds her low rich voice to the boy's and finally all the townsfolk join in and hum. The Chorus enters.

Epilogue

CHORUS
> Many testified to having seen
> The scarlet letter's likeness on the breast
> Of the unhappy minister. Still others
> Firmly disagreed that there was any brand
> Upon his hallow'd body. But all acknowledg'd
> That their most reverend minister had no
> Relation to the guilt of Hester Prynne.
> Rather conscious he was dying, Arthur
> Dimmesdale made his death a parable: that 'fore
> Infinite Purity, we are sinners all.

A bell begins to toll. Quietly at first but ever louder throughout.

> Old Roger Chillingsworth, bereft of his
> Revenge, shrank from sight like weed uprooted
> Withers in the noonday sun. Upon his death
> Bequeath'd the daughter of one Mistress Prynne

---

[3] The hymn is in praise of God and reminiscent of traditional homophonic chorales such as the "Doxology" or "All People That On Earth Do Dwell." See Appendix, p. 89 for details.

CHORUS (*cont'd.*)
> Such property in England to make her heiress
> And in marriage worthy of the noblest hand.

Crossing down center.

> After many absent years, Hester
> Prynne return'd to Boston. Here had been
> Her sin and here would be her penitence.
> She liv'd her life in solitude consoling
> Those in need and showing by example
> How sacred love should bring us peace.
> A simple slab of slate marks where she rests
> Not far from her beloved minister.
> A monument that we might live the better,
> By lessons learn'd from this the scarlet letter.

The people sing out the last chorus as townsmen pick up the deceased minister. The bell rings loudly, supported by a sustained organ note. Upstage, the colossal center doors swing open, revealing a blinding light into which the mourners process. Hester takes Dimmesdale's hand as she and Pearl accompany the body. Pearl looks back toward the Chorus, who, as the lights fade, lays a white rose down center. The bell tolls. Darkness. Silence.

END OF PLAY

෨෬

APPENDIX

If the actress playing Hester Prynne cannot sing, she could be interrupted in ACT TWO, Scene Four before commencing the song by Pearl's questioning and by Dimmesdale's entrance. However, having a song is much preferred, one composed in Elizabethan times such as "What If A Day," the full score of which appears on pages 90 and 91.

The final anthem should be a hymn in the manner of the common "Doxology" or "All People That On Earth Do Dwell" or even "Praise Be To Him, The Almighty" that can have an elegiac feel in its adoration.

In the mid 16th Century, Louis Bourgeois joined the Protestant Reformer John Calvin in Geneva and together they compiled the *Geneva Psalter*. The melody Bourgeois composed for the 100th Psalm has become the most famous of all Protestants hymns. Commonly known as "Old 100th," the melody is the basis for today's Protestant "Doxology." When the Puritans landed in Plymouth in 1620, they brought copies of *The Book of Psalmes*, which Henry Ainsworth had printed for use by the fugitive congregations in Holland. Ainsworth's translation was much closer to Calvin's rendition than the modern "Doxology," and appears below.

PSALM 100
("Doxology")

SHOWT TO JEHOVAH, ALL THE EARTH;
SERVE YE JEHOVAH WITH GLADNESS;
BEFORE HIM COME WITH SINGING MIRTH;
KNOW THAT JEHOVAH HE GOD IS

What if a day

Time of Elizabeth

In moderate time

1. What if a day, or a month, or a year, Crown thy de-lights with a
2. Earth's but a point of the world, and a man Is but a point of the

thousand sweet con-tent-ings, a thousand sweet con - tent - ings?
Earth's compar - ed cen - tre, the Earth's compar - ed cen - tre;

May not the change of a night or an hour Cross thy delights with as
Shall then the point of a point be so vain, As to triumph in a

90

many sad tormentings, as man-y sad tor-ment-ings? For-tune, hon-our,
sil-ly point's ad-venture, a sil-ly point's ad-ven-ture? All in haz-ard

beau-ty, youth, Are but blossoms dy-ing; Wan-ton pleasure,
that we have, Here is nothing bid-ing; Days of pleasure

dot-ing love, Are but shad-ows fly-ing. All our joys
are as streams Thro' fair meadows glid-ing. Weal or woe,

are but toys, I-dle thoughts de-ceiv-ing. None hath pow'r
time doth go, Time hath no re-turn-ing; Se-cret fates

of an hour Of the life's be-reav-ing.
guide our states Both in mirth and mourn-ing.